How to Overcome

Being talks on Judges

J T Mawson

Scripture Truth Publications

HOW TO OVERCOME

First published 1912 in paperback by R.Besley, 12 Paternoster Row, London, E.C. (& G.E. Mawson, 133 Arncliffe Terrace, Bradford) and in hardback in "Every Christian's Library or, The Bible Lover's Bookshelf" by Pickering & Inglis, Printers and Publishers, Glasgow (& Alfred Holness, 14 Paternoster Row, E.C.; Gospel Publishing House (D.T.Bass), Binghampton, New York)

Second edition published 1929 by The Central Bible Truth Depôt, 5 Rose Street, London, E.C.4

Third edition published 1936 by Central Bible Truth Depôt, 5 Rose Street, London, E.C.4

Fourth edition published c1965 by Central Bible Truth Depôt, 11 Little Britain, London, E.C.1

Re-typeset with amended/additional references and Preface from the first edition and transferred to Digital Printing 2009

ISBN: 978-0-901860-62-0 (paperback)

Copyright © 2009 Scripture Truth Publications

A publication of Scripture Truth

All rights reserved. No part of this publication may be reproduced, stored in a retrieval system, or transmitted, in any form or by any means, electronic, mechanical, photocopying, recording or otherwise without prior permission of Scripture Truth Publications.

Scripture quotations, unless otherwise indicated, are taken from The Authorized (King James) Version ("AV"). Rights in the Authorized Version are vested in the Crown. Reproduced by permission of the Crown's patentee, Cambridge University Press.

Scripture quotations marked "N.Tr." are taken from "The Holy Scriptures, a NewTranslation from the Original Languages" by J. N. Darby (G Morrish, 1890)

Cover photograph ©iStockphoto.com/Ynot2 (Gilad Levy)

Published by Scripture Truth Publications
31-33 Glover Street,
Crewe, Cheshire, CW1 3LD

Scripture Truth is an imprint of Central Bible Hammond Trust, a charitable trust

Typesetting by John Rice
Printed and bound by Lightning Source

Preface to 2009 Edition

This edition contains the re-typeset text of the second and subsequent editions, together with the Preface from the first edition. In checking the text, reference has been made to all previous editions.

A few spelling and quotation corrections were necessary. To assist the twenty-first century reader, minor changes in presentation have been made. The use of quotation (speech) marks has been updated. In Scripture references the full title of the book is provided, to facilitate ease of lookup. Some references have been added to scriptures quoted because not all today are as familiar with the Bible as those of J T Mawson's generation. Otherwise the text has not been changed.

Every Christian is called to be an *overcomer*. But how? Using examples from the books of Judges (and Ruth) the author identifies the Christian's enemies and the way to gain victory over each one. Whether we realise it or not, the battle is on!

The publishers commend this book to you. May it help you to experience the joy of victory day by day.

John Rice

HOW TO OVERCOME

Contents

    Preface to 2009 Edition 3
    Preface to First Edition by J. Wilson Smith . 7
1. Foreword 9
2. How to Overcome the World 23
3. How to Overcome the Flesh 41
4. How to Overcome the Devil 63
5. How to Overcome Earthly Things 87
6. How to Overcome Carnal Religion 107
7. Delivered and Devoted 131

HOW TO OVERCOME

Preface to the First Edition

The history of the ways of God's people is, alas, one of chronic failure; and hence we read, as to Israel, that "for about the time of forty years suffered He their manners in the wilderness": and again, after that, "about the space of four hundred and fifty years He gave them Judges until Samuel the prophet"; but their manners during this latter space were as provocative to God, if not more so, than during the former.

The book of Judges comes between that of Joshua (at the close of which we read of his death, and of "the bones of Joseph", and also of the death of Eleazar the high priest) and the Book of Ruth, which has for its last word, the significant name of David, the man after God's own heart. Without a Joseph, a Joshua and an Eleazar — three departed leaders — what should the people have done but depend the more on God as their only, but perfect, source of strength and victory? They did the very opposite and had to suffer accordingly. They forsook the Lord and worshipped idols, becoming the slaves of their varied oppressors. They sank lower and lower until God was "grieved for the misery of Israel". Oft did He interpose and send judge after judge who acted for Him and delivered the captives; but as oft did they rebel and suffer again, until the period closes in hopeless national corruption.

But just then, we find a praying mother and Samuel for an answer; and thereafter a David and a Kingdom established. This was God's gracious interposition: and with a king and a leader, none need do any longer that which was "right in his own eyes".

The parallel between those days and our own is easily seem. We are in Laodicean surroundings, and may well walk humbly: but we await the coming of our Lord from Heaven, whose advent shall bring to a close the chequered history of His Church here below; when He shall present her to Himself a glorious Church without spot or wrinkle or any such thing, and when grace shall gain the victory.

Meantime His grace faileth not. May all His people be strong in that grace while they have to contend, as good soldiers of Jesus Christ, with every form of spiritual evil. The following pages will be found a fitting stimulus in this conflict, and will be scanned with growing interest by the diligent reader.

J. Wilson Smith

Chapter 1
Foreword

THE IMPRISONED EAGLE

I saw a pathetic sight in Scotland. It was a great eagle in a massive cage. The sun shining brilliantly in the heavens seemed to be calling to it to rise from the earth and rejoice in its natural element, and the royal bird in response to the call fixed its eye on the sun and spread its mighty wings and stooped for flight, and then, becoming conscious of the iron bars that held it prisoner, it dropped its wings and lowered its head in apparent disappointment and shame. I watched that captive bird on that lovely summer afternoon with growing interest. Again and again the light flashed in its eyes as it faced the sun and lifted its wings in the futile endeavour to soar away to the upper air, and just as often its wings sank down and it bowed its neck; the most striking figure of depression and defeat that I had ever looked upon. Had I been an artist and had I wished to paint a picture of defeat, that great bird would have been my model. And yet it had the *desire* for liberty, that was clear in the flashing eye, and it had *power* for liberty, that was clear in the outstretched pinions; it was the cage that held it prisoner in spite of its desire and in spite of the power.

The captive bird became a parable to me. It spoke to me of Christians, and, alas! how many such there are, who have the *desire* for the things above, where Christ sitteth on the right hand of God (Colossians 3:1), and these things are their own things, for they have been freely given to them of God, and the Divine nature is in them, or they would not be Christians at all. They have the *power* also to rise up in thought and affection to where their true life is, for the Holy Spirit dwells in them, and yet as to the practical enjoyment of these things they know nothing. Some of them did once, perhaps, but not now, for they are held as prisoners to the earth. They are encaged who should be free.

These captive Christians are not happy. They get glimpses of the glory that shines in the face of Jesus, and their hearts are stirred, and they vow that they will be free, but sighs instead of songs break from their sad hearts and they confess to themselves, even if they hide it from others, the completeness of their bondage. They sometimes toss upon their beds with regrets and groans and prayers, but they find that their resolutions are unavailing. The snares with which the devil enticed them have become a cage in which he holds them, and they despair of ever feeling the thrill of joy of Christian liberty again.

Let it be freely owned, as it has been fully proved, that there never was any satisfaction or profit to any Christian in worldly or fleshly things, they only bring strife into the soul and bitter regrets into the heart, and make the unhappy Christian the captive of the things that he has tried. Yet is there no way of deliverance? and shall the captive never become an overcomer? Yes, there is hope, for the Lord is gracious, and there is a way of deliverance for those who feel their bondage. "Those vows in the night, so fierce" and apparently so unavailing, show that the life of the soul has not been utterly crushed. They prove that there is a faithful Advocate with the Father, Jesus Christ the righteous, who is the propitiation for our sins; they prove also that there is a faithful Holy Spirit within the soul, for He it is that creates the exercise within it, so that the sighing of the prisoner goes up to God. And because of these things, and because it is God's will that His children should be free from every yoke of bondage, we turn to this Old Testament Book to learn, How to Overcome.

We need the whole Bible: to neglect any part of it means certain loss. The Old Testament is as necessary as the New, for in the New it is declared that the things which are recorded in the Old Testament were written for our admonition (1 Corinthians 10:11).

The largest nugget that the Californian gold-fields ever yielded was found upon a claim which was supposed to be worked out. The Bible is supposed by some to be worked out, good enough for former days, but out of date and of no practical value now, and so they have abandoned it for other fields that yield no gold at all. We know that it is an inexhaustible mine of wealth, for it is the word of the living God.

It is with this knowledge that we turn to the Book of Judges. We are not concerned as to what human hand held the pen in the writing of it; it is sufficient that it has its place in the Scriptures, and "all Scripture is given by inspiration of God … that the man of God may be perfect, throughly furnished unto all good works" (2 Timothy 3:16-17).

There is in the Book of Judges the dark background of the failures and defeats of Israel. Solemn warnings indeed are they all to us, for we are in danger of being overcome and enthralled by foes not one whit less real than were those that enslaved God's people of old. But this dark background does but throw into bright relief the great victories gained by men whose faith was in God. These victories are illustrative of the way in which we, by the grace of God, may also overcome.

So the title of our talks shall be "How to Overcome", and the foes of which we will speak are:—

The Mesopotamians	THE WORLD.
The Moabites	THE FLESH.
The Canaanites	THE DEVIL.
The Midianites	EARTHLY THINGS.
The Philistines	CARNAL RELIGION.

It is in the foregoing order that they are presented to us and in that order we will consider them, with the earnest prayer that we may all be more than conquerors through Him that loved us (Romans 8:37).

We shall have little difficulty in proving that the nations that oppressed Israel set forth our foes as already stated, for the marks are so evident upon the face of them; nor shall we find many who will quarrel with us when we assert that the majority of Christians are under the power of one or more of these foes, and that the crying need of the day is deliverance.

THE CHARACTER OF THE VICTORIES

The victories gained by the Judges were not aggressive in their character; they were not the victories of conquest. Their foes sought to quench their light as a free nation, and to rob them of the inheritance which God had given them, and every battle that these leaders in Israel fought was to maintain their national existence, and to retain and enjoy that which belonged to them.

It was God's intention that these people should be ever victorious; when they crossed the Jordan He was with them in all the power of His might, and had they continued in subjection to Him no other yoke could have been placed upon their necks. But they turned away from Him and had to reap the bitter fruits of their backslidings. They followed the sins and gods of the nations, and they became the slaves of that which they followed. Now it is the same God, who, in those times which are past, overthrew the Egyptians and gave the promised land to Israel, that has now wrought deliverance for us and given us an inheritance incorruptible and which fadeth not away. It is this which the gospel proclaims, and all who have received it can rejoice in a great Saviour, who "through death [has] destroy[ed] him that had the power of death, that is, the devil; and deliver[ed] them who through fear of death were all their lifetime subject to bondage" (Hebrews 2:14-15). And this deliverance from the power of the devil has been effected that we might enter upon and enjoy the great riches which have been given to us in and with Christ.

But we are exhorted to stand fast in this liberty wherewith we have been made free, for the danger of being entangled with some yoke of bondage is ever present. It is when we fail in this, and the heart goes after the things of the world and the flesh, that we become enslaved, and, like these sons of Jacob, we become the servants of that which we follow. Then is all service and witness hindered; we become wretched ourselves and useless to others.

But as we stand fast in our God-given liberty, with single eye and undivided heart, we are able to fulfil our high destiny as witnesses for Christ, and to win fresh territory for Him; for every soul saved by our testimony is a fresh bit of territory won from the power of the enemy, for the Lord's kingdom and glory.

The secret of Christian liberty

The gospel has set us free from the yoke of sin and Satan that we might "yield ourselves to God" (Romans 6:13). This is the secret of a happy life of Christian liberty, for as we yield our necks to His yoke we shall be free from all others. And this yoke is not irksome but easy, for in yielding ourselves to God, we are yielding to the One whose measureless love has been manifested towards us in the death of Jesus. The blood through which we have redemption is the pledge and token to us of a love too vast to comprehend, and the knowledge of that love constrains us not to live unto ourselves but unto Him whose love it is.

A notable feature

There is a notable feature in Israel's history at this time which demands attention. It is stated (1 Kings 6:1) that the number of years between the deliverance from Egypt and the building of Solomon's temple was 480 years. But the actual number according to Paul's address to the Jews (Acts 13) was 573, showing a difference of 93 years in the two accounts.

How can the Book be of divine origin when such a glaring discrepancy occurs in it? sneers the infidel — a discrepancy which ordinary human care might have avoided.

But that over which the infidel in his blindness stumbles is full of instruction to those who are willing to be taught of God, and in this, which seems to be an error, we have a solemn lesson.

The building of Solomon's temple runs on the line of God's intentions for His people. He had redeemed them that they might live wholly unto Himself and prepare for Him a habitation (Exodus 15:2). But during the ninety-three years in which they served His enemies and theirs, they were not living unto Him — this was not His purpose for them — and, as a consequence, He could not reckon these sad years in His calendar.

In Acts 13 the Apostle Paul pressed upon the people the fact that Christ was their only hope. He showed them that all apart from Him had failed. Even David, their greatest deliverer and boast, had fallen under the power of death and saw corruption. This was the line of their responsibility, and the years of failure are reckoned, that the risen Christ, in His perfection and victory over all the foes, might stand out in blessed contrast to all that had passed before Him.

The ninety-three years omitted from God's reckoning, when it was a question of *His purpose for His people*, seem to be made up as follows:

8	years under Mesopotamia	(chapter 3:8).
18	years under Moab	(chapter 3:14).
20	years under Canaan	(chapter 4:3).
7	years under Midian	(chapter 6:1).
40	years under Philistia	(chapter 13:1).
93		

We have, in addition to the above, the oppression of the Amorites for eighteen years (chapter 10:8), but here it is distinctly stated to have been on the other side of Jordan only (not truly in the land), and so does not affect the question at all.

If this is the true explanation for the apparent discrepancy (and we believe it to be so), what a weighty lesson it teaches. All the days and years which are not lived unto God are lost days, and we do not truly live unto Him if we are held in bondage by our foes. We can only be said to live truly unto Him as our souls are free and Christ and His things are supreme in our lives. All else is death and loss.

This will all be manifested at the judgment seat of Christ, when every man's work will be tried. We shall see then, that every day in which we have lived for the world, the flesh, the devil, or for anything instead of Christ, has been a lost day. "If any man's work shall be burned, he shall suffer loss: but he himself shall be saved; yet so as by fire" (1 Corinthians 3:15).

Let us give earnest heed to this all-important matter, remembering that the days are few. The coming of the Lord is at hand, when we shall be swept by His redemptive power into the eternal felicity of our Fatherland, and, as we look back upon the path we have trodden, we shall be compelled then to write L-O-S-T upon every day and hour in which Christ has not been first in our lives, for then we shall see things as God sees them.

It is evident, then, that to live unto Him is the only life worth living, for this alone will remain for eternity. The world thinks differently, and the flesh within us may make other suggestions, and propose self-indulgence, ease, worldliness, fame, gold or pleasure as being more worthy of our attention; but deep down in our hearts we know better, and taught by the Spirit we clearly see that the great works of men will come to naught, while labour in the Lord is not in vain; the earth also and the works therein shall perish, while our inheritance and the things of God are precious, imperishable and eternal.

HOLD THE FORT

It is possible for every child of God to carry the war into the enemy's camp as a good soldier of Jesus Christ, and to follow boldly the unfurled standard of the testimony of our Lord; but this, which is true Christian warfare, is scarcely within the scope of our talks. It is only as the victories of which we speak are gained that we can take up the sword aggressively.

In overcoming the world, etc., we are "holding the fort" against foes that seek a footing within our hearts in order to make us useless for the Lord. We are, in short, *"keeping ourselves for Christ"*.

We may feel our weakness, and our inability to do anything for the Saviour whom we love, but we can all keep ourselves for Him alone, and anything is possible to those who do this. But to do this we must keep the line of communication with Himself intact.

As a general leads his men against the enemy he must keep in constant communication with the base of his supplies. He will be a beaten man if he does not, for food, ammunition and reinforcements and everything he needs are at the base. The foe will use every means in his power to outflank him and to cut the line of his communications. He must guard that line at all costs; if he is careless as to this the valour and enthusiasm of his men will be in vain.

We, too, must keep in touch with our base if we are to be victorious. The devil is a wily foe and will cut us off from our supplies if he can, hence the need of the exhortation: "Cleave to the Lord with purpose of heart" (Acts 11:23), for all our supplies are in Him. He is indispensable to us, but He is all-sufficient for us, and we cannot fail if we cleave to Him. Our business is to —

"Yield ourselves unto God" (Romans 6:13).

"Cleave unto the Lord" (Acts 11:23).

"Walk in the Spirit" (Galatians 5:16, 25).

So shall we be more than conquerors through Him that loved us.

Mesopotamia: Type of The World

"And the children of Israel dwelt among the Canaanites, Hittites, and Amorites, and Perizzites, and Hivites, and Jebusites: and they took their daughters to be their wives, and, gave their daughters to their sons, and served their gods. And the children of Israel did evil in the sight of the LORD, and forgat the LORD their God, and served Baalim and the groves. Therefore the anger of the LORD was hot against Israel, and he sold them into the hand of Chushan-rishathaim king of Mesopotamia: and the children of Israel served Chushan-rishathaim eight years. And when the children of Israel cried unto the LORD, the LORD raised up a deliverer to the children of Israel, who delivered them, even Othniel the son of Kenaz, Caleb's younger brother. And the Spirit of the LORD came upon him, and he judged Israel, and went out to war: and the LORD delivered Chushan-rishathaim king of Mesopotamia into his hand; and his hand prevailed against Chushan-rishathaim. And the land had rest forty years. And Othniel the son of Kenaz died."

JUDGES 3:5-11

THE WORLD

"And afterward the children of Judah went down to fight against the Canaanites, that dwelt in the mountain, and in the south, and in the valley. And Judah went against the Canaanites that dwelt in Hebron: (now the name of Hebron before was Kirjath-arba): and they slew Sheshai, and Ahiman, and Talmai. And from thence he went against the inhabitants of Debir: and the name of Debir before was Kirjath-sepher: And Caleb said, He that smiteth Kirjath-sepher, and taketh it, to him will I give Achsah my daughter to wife. And Othniel the son of Kenaz, Caleb's younger brother took it: and he gave him Achsah his daughter to wife. And it came to pass, when she came to him, that she moved him to ask of her father a field: and she lighted from off her ass; and Caleb said unto her, What wilt thou? And she said unto him, Give me a blessing: for thou hast given me a south land; give me also springs of water. And Caleb gave her the upper springs and the nether springs."

JUDGES 1:9-15

HOW TO OVERCOME

Chapter 2
How to Overcome the World

WHAT IS THE WORLD?

Mesopotamia is a type of the world; not in its material character, which our eyes can see, but of its principles and ways, motives and maxims, which govern and control men who are not subject to God. The material world is the sphere in which these things find play, and the pomp and glory of it are the product of the will of men, but the will of men and their efforts for their own pleasure and exaltation are the spirit and life of it, while the material world is but the shell.

The world in this character is opposed to God; it is like a stronghold that harbours rebels against their rightful sovereign, and all who are on good terms with it are against God, for we read: "The friendship of the world is enmity with God; whosoever therefore will be a friend of the world is the enemy of God" (James 4:4). It appeals to the lusts within men, and is summed up for us in the verse: "For all that is in the world, the lust of the flesh, the lust of the eyes, and the pride of life, is not of the Father, but is of the world" (1 John 2:16). It is evident that it has nothing in common with God. Whether it is cultured or debased, religious or profane, it is His great rival, holding, by its magnetic power, the hearts of men which ought to be yielded up to God.

THE THREE GREAT FEATURES OF THE WORLD

The three great features of the world appeared first in the temptation in the Garden of Eden. Under the malign power of Satan, Eve saw that the forbidden tree was —

(1) Good for food — Lust of the flesh:
(2) Pleasant to the eyes — Lust of the eyes:
(3) And a tree to be desired to make one wise — Pride of life (Genesis 3:6):

and, like leaves swept by the whirlwind from the tree that gave them life, the woman and then the man were swept far from God by this attack of the enemy. God was dethroned in their hearts; self became the centre of their lives. From that time onward man has been controlled by lust for what he has not, and pride in what he has; and we see in Cain and his descendants that it became easy for men to make temporary happiness for themselves apart from God and in independence of Him (Genesis 4:16-22).

ABRAM WAS CALLED OUT OF MESOPOTAMIA

It was out of Mesopotamia that Abram was called by God (Genesis 12:1). And the call of Abram is figurative of the call of men by the gospel today. The great object of the gospel is not to uplift or improve the world (though the world would be a sorry place without it), but to deliver men from its seductions, and call them out of it unto God. It is the will of God that His people should be delivered from its bondage and power, but for this there had to be a great sacrifice. That sacrifice has been made, for our

THE WORLD

Lord Jesus Christ "gave Himself for our sins, that He might deliver us from this present evil world, according to the will of God and our Father: to whom be glory for ever" (Galatians 1:4-5). The gospel of God's grace, which tells of the great sacrifice which love has made, is a delivering gospel; it sets men free from the delusions and allurements of a world that is doomed to judgment and gives them heavenly hopes. It links them up with heaven, so that heaven becomes their Fatherland and home. "Blessed be the God and Father of our Lord Jesus Christ, which according to His abundant mercy hath begotten us again unto a lively hope by the resurrection of Jesus Christ from the dead, To an inheritance incorruptible, and undefiled, and that fadeth not away, reserved in heaven for you" (1 Peter 1:3-4).

Heaven is the home of all those who have believed the gospel, and just in the measure in which we realize this shall we be strangers and pilgrims in the world.

Now God called Abram out of Mesopotamia that henceforward he and his descendants might be His own people; and, having obeyed the call of God, it is evident that the king of that land had no further claim over them. It is equally evident that those who have believed the gospel and belong to Christ are not of the world, for He has said: "They are not of the world, even as I am not of the world" (John 17:14). But Israel departed from God, and in so doing exchanged the joy and liberty of serving Him for bitter slavery; and the first king under whose yoke they came was Chushan-rishathaim, king of the land out of which Abram had been called. In like manner, oftentimes, Christians turn from the true fountain of life and gladness to seek satisfaction in this world, and that which they seek and follow enslaves them, and they lose their liberty and joy. We are all in danger of this, and need to give heed to the exhortation: "Love not the world, neither the things that are in the world" (1 John 2:15).

THE KING OF MESOPOTAMIA

The name of the king means "double-wickedness", and in this it is a true type of the world, for we know that the one who controls the world is the devil (1 John 5:19). Behind the scenes he holds sway: he offered all the glory of its kingdoms to the Lord: he still offers these things to the children of men, and by the glitter of them bewitches and destroys their souls. His wickedness in this respect has a double character, for he is both the god and the prince of the world which he controls (John 12:31; 2 Corinthians 4:4).

The Israelites began to feel the iron yoke to which they had become subject, and they cried unto the Lord in their distress. He heard their cries and raised up for them a deliverer who was more than a match for all the power of Mesopotamia.

THE DELIVERER

The man whom God could use to set His people free was named Othniel, which means, "powerful man of God". He is introduced to our notice in chapter 1. There his valour was fully tested and proved, and was also rewarded by the hand of the daughter of Caleb, and with her he received the south land — the sunny and fruitful place — and with this south land the upper and nether springs.

It was the man who possessed as his inheritance the south land, with the upper and nether springs that overcame the Mesopotamians.

It is God's way in these bright days of grace to work by the law of attraction. He would draw us from what is evil by the mighty magnetism of His goodness and love, and would drive the world from our hearts by the expulsive power of some better thing. This better thing is the south land with its upper and nether springs.

The South land

The radiant beauty of this wonderful inheritance unfolds before our vision in the Gospel of John; and in John's writings, more often than in any other part of Scripture, we are warned against the world; for that which God has for us and the world are in perpetual antagonism. They cannot be blended or reconciled.

Now the Gospel of John possesses a very peculiar character. In it the Lord is not presented to us as the poor Man without a place to lay His head, but as "The only-begotten Son, which is in the bosom of the Father" (chapter 1:18). That was His home, His rest, and His place of joy. He was able to speak of His possession in the hearing of His disciples, *and the characteristic word of the Gospel is the possessive pronoun "My"*. In chapters 14-17 the Lord uses it about thirty times. He was there in the midst of His prized possessions — the things that He could call His own: "My Father's house". "My Father", "My joy", "My way", "My name", "My peace", "My glory", and so forth. It is our blessed privilege to behold Him, as the Only-begotten rejoicing in the perennial sunshine of His inheritance. But He came into this world in order to seek out and find companions, who should share these things with Him for ever.

Now Christianity is not made up of dogma and creed only, it is real and living, and consists in the enjoyment of these things of which the Lord here speaks.

He would have all whom He can call His own enjoy these things, for He said: "My peace I give unto you" (chapter

14:27). "These things have I spoken unto you, that My joy might remain in you" (chapter 15:11). "The glory which Thou hast given Me I have given them" (chapter 17:22, N.Tr.). "My Father and your Father, ... My God and your God" (chapter 20:17, N.Tr.). That these things might be ours He has associated us with Himself as His brethren, and it is His delight to give to us, not as the world giveth, but to share with us this wonderful inheritance. He has brought us to Himself that we might know and enjoy the best of His portion, even His Father's love; for He prayed to His Father that "the world might know that Thou hast ... loved them, as Thou hast loved Me" (chapter 17:23). And again, "I have declared unto them Thy name, and will declare it: that the love wherewith Thou hast loved Me may be in them, and I in them" (chapter 17:26).

Here we are brought to the infinitude and eternity of divine love, too vast for our poor minds to comprehend; but, though we have scarcely begun to understand the precious meaning of the words, we are conscious that they are indeed the words of eternal life, and the sound of them thrills our hearts and makes them throb, responsive to this unmeasured love.

How we may enjoy this Inheritance

Now we can understand the Lord rejoicing in this south land where all is of God, for He was the Son of God, but how can we understand or enjoy this place which He gives us in association with Himself?

If the King of these realms went down to a convict prison and pardoned a criminal there, that would be an act of clemency; but it would not be a kindness if he took him to his palace as a companion. The man would be quite out of place there, and probably far happier in the prison than in the palace. But if the King could give to him the spirit of one of his children, then all would be changed, for the man would then be able to appreciate the things of the King and would be at home in his company. Now what the King could never do God has done. He has given to us the Spirit of His Son — the Holy Ghost — and the Spirit not only enables us to cry, "Abba, Father", but reveals to us the things of Christ, and enables us to enjoy them, and *in the Spirit thus given to us we have the upper and nether springs.*

We shall enjoy this place of blessing in all its fulness when we reach the Father's house on high, but such is His love to us that He will not keep us waiting for this joy until we reach that blest abode; He has given to us His Spirit that we might begin to enjoy it now.

THE WORLD'S RESOURCES

Mesopotamia means "the land of two rivers", and this is another feature which marks it out as being figurative of the world. It would be wrong to suppose that the world has nothing to offer, for it has two streams which, in its eyes, are both noble and sufficient. But they are not what they seem to be; they cannot yield that which the heart craves; and yet men, refusing the truth, blindly seek after them, even as Naaman in his pride cried: "Are not Abana and Pharpar, rivers of Damascus, better than all the waters of Israel?" The two great streams of which the world boasts are exposed in their unsatisfying character in John's Gospel. They are the counterfeit of what God has for men, and are: (1) Pleasure (chapter 4) and (2) Religion (chapter 7). The two sides of man's nature are appealed to, but of the first the Lord of Truth said: "Whosoever drinketh of this water shall thirst again" (chapter 4:13). And on the great day of the greatest religious festival Jesus looked with compassion upon the unsatisfied multitude, and cried: "If any man thirst" (chapter 7:37).

As all the rivers run into the sea, and yet the sea is not full, so all the waters of this world's resources may flow into the heart of man and he remains unsatisfied. His heart is too big for the world; for he was created for God, and God alone can satisfy his thirst. The world's pleasure is totally inadequate to give him lasting joy, and its religion cannot save or uplift his soul.

The Lord's Proposals — The upper and nether springs

How blessed it is to find the Lord prepared to satisfy alike the heart-thirst of the pleasure-seeker, and to fill up the breasts of those who prove how unable to fill them were all the festivities of a hollow religion. He proposes to make men independent of the world in these wonderful words: "Whosoever drinketh of this water shall thirst again: but whosoever drinketh of the water that I shall give him shall never thirst; but the water that I shall give him shall be in him a well of water springing up into everlasting life" (John 4:13-14). In like manner He also proposes to make them contributors to the deep need of thirsty hearts within the world, for "In the last day, that great day of the feast, Jesus stood and cried, saying, If any man thirst, let him come unto Me, and drink. He that believeth on Me, as the Scripture hath said, out of his belly shall flow rivers of living water. But this spake He of the Spirit, which they that believe on Him should receive: for the Holy Ghost was not yet given: because that Jesus was not yet glorified" (John 7:37-39). Could anything be more magnificent than this? To have a deep well-spring of satisfaction within, springing up into everlasting life — rising up to its Source and Giver in intelligent appreciation and worship — this is the upper spring; and then, to have these same waters of refreshing flowing out in rivers to others for their blessing also — this is the nether spring.

These things are no mere fancy; it is true that they surpass the highest dreams of the poet, but they are, nevertheless, the solid truths of God, and are very tangible and real to those who love Him.

It is not difficult to see that as the heart enjoys this wonderful inheritance the world will have no charms. Its smiles will not allure, nor its frowns dismay: the bands of it will be loosened, and the soul free from it.

Only those who possess and enjoy this inheritance are true Othniels — men of God — free themselves, and delivering others also.

But it is not by the energy of nature or by great efforts on our part to deny ourselves that we overcome the world; all such efforts would merely end in miserable legality and failure. It is as we enter by faith upon these things, and the heart truly enjoys them, that we shall delight in the commandments of the Lord, and prove that His commandments are not grievous. "For whatsoever is born of God overcometh the world: and this is the victory that overcometh the world, even our faith. Who is he that overcometh the world, but he that believeth that Jesus is the Son of God?" (1 John 5:4-5).

Our great Example

There has been but one perfect Man upon the earth, who in dependence upon God trod an ever-victorious path, and He has left us an example that we should walk in His steps. If we love Him, we shall delight to follow Him, and shall prove that His yoke is easy and His burden light. The Gospel of Luke presents the Lord to us in the particularly attractive character of the Man in dependence upon God, and it is in that Gospel that the devil confronted Him with the threefold temptation which had wrought such disaster in Eden.

The temptation in the wilderness (Luke 4:1-13) consisted in:

(1) The lust of the flesh — make these stones into bread.

(2) The lust of the eye — all the kingdoms of the world.

(3) The pride of life — cast Thyself down hence.

The first attack was met by a perfect answer: "It is written, That man shall not live by bread alone, but by every word of GOD." Certainly the Lord had the power to make stones into bread, but He was here to do God's will alone, and He never used His power on His own behalf; moreover, He would not look to the earth for His satisfaction but to God. He did not seek sustenance from below but from above.

"GOD" filled His heart, and was His answer to the devil's temptation. God would supply His every need, and He would not use His own power to take Himself out of the place of entire dependence on God. He was not here to please Himself but to do the will of God; the lust of the flesh had no place in His heart. It was here that Adam and Eve failed: they put self before God, but where they were overthrown Jesus stood firm, and the devil was foiled and driven back.

The attack was renewed from another quarter, and all the splendours of the world's kingdoms were set before His eye: but the power and pomp and greatness which dazzle and fascinate men, and for which they will sell their souls and deny their God had no charm for Jesus. Palmerston, the great Prime Minister, than whom none knew men better, said: "Every man has his price"; but here was One whom no inducement could turn aside from His purpose. His eyes were upon God, and He met the trial with the conclusive answer: "For it is written, Thou shalt worship the Lord thy GOD, and Him only shalt thou serve." A true worshipper of God is one whose heart is filled with His glory. It was ever so with Jesus here upon earth, and in that filled heart there was no room for the world; its empty splendour did not attract Him. "GOD" was also His answer to the second temptation.

Yet again the devil returned to the attack and suggested that He should cast Himself down from the temple pinnacle in the presence of the multitude below, and by so doing prove Himself to be the Son of God — the object of God's special care according to His word. But the trap was laid in vain: Jesus would await God's time for the manifestation of Himself and His glory. He would not tempt God by taking matters into His own hands and vindicating Himself, so he replied, "It is said, Thou shalt not tempt the Lord thy GOD."

"GOD" is again the answer of the truly dependent and so ever victorious Man. He was impregnable, for He set the Lord always before Him. He looked to "GOD" for His sustenance. "GOD" filled His heart to the exclusion of all beside. "GOD" was His confidence, so that He left His times entirely in His hands and could not be moved.

Satan returned to the attack when the shadows of the cross were falling darkly on the pathway of the Lord. To turn Him aside from the path of obedience was still the intention of the enemy. He had failed to accomplish this by the attractions and favours of the world so he sought to do it by the terrors and frowns of it (Matthew 16:21).

The Lord began to show His disciples what he must suffer at the hands of men: all the horror of it pressed upon His spirit; and, seizing this opportunity, through Peter, Satan said, "Be it far from Thee [Pity Thyself, AV margin], Lord: this shall not be unto Thee." But the Lord at once detected the foe in His new character of an apparent friend, and He met his subtlety with stern rebuke: "Get thee behind Me, Satan: thou art an offence unto Me: for thou savourest not the things that be of GOD."

"GOD" was still before His blessed soul; His only object for living here. He would not save Himself — that was no business of His — and thus all the devil's great siege guns were brought to bear upon Him in vain: He came through the conflict victoriously. The prince of this world came, but found no vulnerable point: he was utterly defeated. It could not have been otherwise when he tried conclusions with the One whose first recorded words were: "Wist ye not that I must be about My Father's business?"; who lived on account of His Father alone, and never turned to the right hand or the left until He could say, "It is finished."

He overcame the world: its attractions and snares were laid in vain for Him. His heart was satisfied, and every breathing of His soul was controlled by God Himself. He is our Pattern and Guide, and in Him is all the grace and power we need, so that without faltering we may walk in His steps.

We owe everything to the devotion and love of the Lord Jesus Christ, and our hearts have been taught to appreciate Him in whom we have found transcendent beauty. But how did the world treat Him when He manifested Himself in it? They beheld His wondrous works, and were compelled to exclaim: "He hath done all things well." They heard the words of His mouth, and acknowledged:

"Never man spake like this Man." And yet, at the end of it all, they spat in His face, and crowned Him with thorns, and crucified Him between two murderers. There was no room in the world for the lone but lovely Man of Nazareth. He was hated and cast out by it. Keep this in mind, all ye who belong to Him. Remember, also, that the world has never gone in deep contrition to God's footstool, and there expressed its sorrow for this deed; it is still guilty of the blood of God's dear Son. In the presence of this ask yourself the question, What ought to be my attitude towards this world? Can we wonder that Paul should say: "But God forbid that I should glory, save in the cross of our Lord Jesus Christ, by whom the world is crucified unto me, and I unto the world" (Galatians 6:14); or, that it is recorded for our instruction and warning: "Know ye not that the friendship of the world is enmity with God? whosoever therefore will be a friend of the world is the enemy of God" (James 4:4)?

HOW TO OVERCOME

Moab:
Type of The Flesh

"And the children of Israel did evil again in the sight of the LORD: and the LORD strengthened Eglon the king of Moab against Israel, because they had done evil in the sight of the LORD. And he gathered unto him the children of Ammon and Amalek, and went and smote Israel, and possessed the city of palm trees. So the children of Israel served Eglon the king of Moab eighteen years. But when the children of Israel cried unto the LORD, the LORD raised them up a deliverer, Ehud, the son of Gera, a Benjamite, a man left-handed: and by him the children of Israel sent a present unto Eglon, the king of Moab. But Ehud made him a dagger which had two edges, of a cubit length; and he did gird it under his raiment upon his right thigh. And he brought the present unto Eglon king of Moab: and Eglon was a very fat man. And when he had made an end to offer the present, he sent away the people that bare the present. But he himself turned again from the quarries that were by Gilgal, and said, I have a secret errand unto thee, O king: who said, Keep silence. And all that stood by him went out from him. And Ehud came unto him; and he was sitting in a summer parlour which he had for himself alone. And Ehud said, I have a message from God unto thee. And he arose out of his seat. And Ehud put forth his left hand, and took the dagger from his right thigh, and thrust it into his belly: and the haft also went in after the blade; and the fat closed upon the blade, so that he could not draw the dagger out of his belly; and the dirt came out.

THE FLESH

Then Ehud went forth through the porch, and shut the doors of the parlour upon him, and locked them. When he was gone out, his servants came; and when they saw that, behold, the doors of the parlour were locked, they said, Surely he covereth his feet in his summer chamber. And they tarried till they were ashamed: and, behold, he opened not the doors of the parlour; therefore they took a key, and opened them: and, behold, their lord was fallen down dead on the earth. And Ehud escaped while they tarried, and passed beyond the quarries, and escaped into Seirath. And it came to pass, when he was come, that he blew a trumpet in the mountain of Ephraim, and the children of Israel went down with him from the mount, and he before them. And he said unto them, Follow after me: for the Lord hath delivered your enemies the Moabites into your hand. And they went down after him, and took the fords of Jordan toward Moab, and suffered not a man to pass over. And they slew of Moab at that time about ten thousand men, all lusty, and all men of valour; and there escaped not a man. So Moab was subdued that day under the hand of Israel. And the land had rest fourscore years."

JUDGES 3:12-30

HOW TO OVERCOME

Chapter 3
How to Overcome the Flesh

WHAT IS THE FLESH?

Our talk on "the flesh" is not about what is physical, the body, but about that evil principle within us which makes SELF the centre of our thoughts and ways instead of GOD. The flesh is opposed to God's will and cannot please Him (Romans 8:8). It is not subject to the law of God, and, if allowed to act, will always serve the law of sin (Romans 7:25). It first appeared in this character when Eve put forth her hand to take the fruit of the forbidden tree, believing that by so doing she would become greater than God had made her. Self was her object in that act instead of God, and since that day all men by nature have been born into this world in the flesh, that is, they are controlled always by love of self instead of by the love of God. This is the nature of every unrenewed man.

But a great change has taken place in those who have believed the gospel of God's grace; they have been born again by God's Spirit, and have received the Holy Ghost. He dwells in them, so that of them it can be said: "Ye are not in the flesh, but in the Spirit, if so be that the Spirit of God dwell in you" (Romans 8:9). They have received a new life and nature which, instead of making self the centre and circumference of all their thoughts, goes out in its desires and hopes to God Himself.

This is the new nature and life which every one of us who is saved has received. But the flesh remains in us, and it is only as we walk in the Spirit that we shall be free from the bondage of its lusts (Galatians 5:16).

The Moabites are a striking figure of the Flesh

(1) Their start was bad (Genesis 19:37).

(2) They were excluded from the congregation of God's people (Deuteronomy 23:3; Nehemiah 13:1).

(3) They were to be utterly destroyed; the last mention of them in Scripture being: "As I live, saith the Lord of hosts ... surely Moab shall be as Sodom ... a perpetual desolation" (Zephaniah 2:9).

With regard to the flesh, we read in the New Testament: "No flesh should glory in His presence" (1 Corinthians 1:29); and in the Old Testament, "The end of all flesh is come before me" (Genesis 6:13).

"For himself alone"

But in the story before us we find other indications confirming the thought that in Eglon and the Moabites we have a type of the flesh. Eglon had his summer palace, a place of ease and pleasure, and he had it for himself alone (chapter 3:20).

Here, in one brief sentence, the whole character of the flesh is disclosed. It is utterly selfish; it has nothing to render to God; every thought, hope and ambition finds self as the pivot; all that it has it has for "self alone". Oh, have you not often found this detestable thing forcing its way to the front when you least expected it? You did a kind act. Love and sympathy formed the motive, but scarcely was the deed performed when there crept in that base thought —"What will they think of ME, now?" You may have been greatly helped in some service to the Lord, but, instead of being humbled by the grace that used you, and giving all the glory to Him who is the source of it, there was the inward vaunting and exulting, as though by your own strength you had accomplished the work. Or, perhaps, the service was a failure, and you became cast down and depressed, not because the Lord had been dishonoured, but because you had not shone as you had hoped to do. Someone else did something better than you, or outstripped you in devotion, knowledge or ability, and thoughts of rivalry and jealousy took possession of you at once. It was the flesh, base and incorrigible, seeking all for "self alone". Oh, that we might get a true glimpse of its utter hatefulness, and turn away from it with loathing.

THE FLESH HAS NO CLAIM UPON THE CHRISTIAN

The Moabites had no true claim upon Israel, and yet we find that Eglon had set up his throne in the city of the palm trees (which was the very gate of the land — the city which God had taken with a mighty hand for His people), and from that place of power he ruled Israel and laid tribute upon them, so that what God alone had a right to claim from them was being rendered up to the king of Moab. How true a picture is this of the state of thousands of Christians. The flesh has no right to rule us, for, "We are debtors, not to the flesh, to live after the flesh" (Romans 8:12). We owe no debt to that evil principle within us which would make self everything to the exclusion of Christ; we have a perfect right to ignore its clamours and to walk in the Spirit; and yet, as Eglon of Moab received from Israel that which God alone could claim, so, alas! do Christians often yield time and thought and strength to the flesh, forgetting all the while that "If ye live after the flesh, ye shall die: but if ye through the Spirit do mortify the deeds of the body, ye shall live" (Romans 8:13).

Let it be again stated and emphasized that, if you are a Christian, the flesh is a usurper if it dominates you, for, "Ye are not in the flesh, but in the Spirit, if so be that the Spirit of God dwell in you" (Romans 8:9). When we believed the gospel of our salvation, the Spirit of God took up His abode in us; and the sealing of the Spirit means that the Lord has claimed that which He has purchased with His own blood. Now the work of the Spirit within us is to displace self and to overthrow for ever the dominion of the flesh by making Christ supreme in our affections.

You may be sure that the flesh will not readily yield up the sceptre, and will ever be on the alert to assert itself. "For the flesh lusteth against the Spirit, and the Spirit against the flesh: and these are contrary the one to the other" (Galatians 5:17).

ALL OUR EFFORTS TO SUBDUE THE FLESH ARE FUTILE

Let us not suppose that the flesh can be improved or made fit for God. It was said of Moab: *"His taste remained in him, and his scent is not changed"* (Jeremiah 48:11). It is also true that, "That which is born of the flesh is flesh" (John 3:6). It may be religionized, but it will remain in independence of, and rebellion against, God. It often intrudes itself in divine things, but even there it will still seek all for "self alone". It cannot be educated, coaxed, or whipped into subjection to the law of God, for its nature is absolutely contrary to that law.

This is a lesson that must be learnt, though the learning of it is always a bitter process. The progress of the lesson is given in Romans 7.

(1) You long to do that which is good, and are sadly *disappointed* when you find that you can only do that which is bad.

(2) You search for the reason and are *disgusted* when you find that from you, that is your flesh, no good thing can come, for the simple reason that no good thing exists in it.

(3) You make great efforts to throw off the terrible incubus, and *despair* fills your heart as you prove them all to be in vain. Then, when you come to your wits' end and give up the struggle, the load is lifted by another hand. The morning breaks and the way of deliverance from the terrible morass in which you had struggled is made plain. But this deliverance can only be reached in God's way.

How the victory is gained

God found a prince in Israel who not only escaped from the yoke of Moab himself, but was able to deliver others also; and in contemplating the ways of Ehud we shall learn the way of deliverance. He was commissioned to carry the tribute of the Israelites to the monarch of Moab, and from what follows we may conclude that this was not pleasant work; he must have felt how degrading a thing it was for God's people to be thus enslaved. There is no victory apart from exercise of soul. If we are content to walk after the things of the flesh, and with the ordinary kind of Christian living that we see all round us, we shall never know the joy and liberty of power over the flesh.

Ehud's name means, "him that praises", and he was a true son of his father Gera, whose name means, "combat or disputings". You may be sure if you are to become "him that praises" in the full gladness of victory, there must be first exercise and conflict of soul; for victory, joy and praise are always the offspring of true soul exercise.

AT THE STONES OF GILGAL

Having delivered himself of his mission to Eglon, Ehud went to the quarries or stones of Gilgal. That was the right place for the man who felt the bondage under which Israel was groaning, and it was the place where such a feeling would be greatly intensified; for it was there that the reproach of Egypt had been rolled away (Joshua 5:9). The people of God had been bondmen in a strange land; but, when they reached Gilgal, they were not only free, but were brought to the land of liberty; circumcision took place there, and *circumcision was the sign of their freedom.*

It was from Gilgal, as God's freedmen, that they had gone to victory after victory; and, if they had not forgotten that place and its lessons, they would never have known defeat and slavery, and the shoutings of victory would never have given place to the lamentations of Bochim.

Ehud, in going to Gilgal, had reached the point of departure; the point, in fact, where the true life began; the life which God intended that the people, whom He had so wonderfully redeemed, should live.

Gilgal was the most interesting spot in the land:

(1) There stood the twelve stones taken out of the bed of Jordan.
(2) There circumcision took place.
(3) The passover was celebrated.
(4) They ate of the old corn of the land.
(5) The Captain of the Lord's host took his place at their head as leader and guide.

We will deal only with the first two of these important events, as they have a more particular bearing on our present subject; and, if they are understood, we shall have little difficulty in comprehending what followed them.

THE TWELVE STONES

These had been taken from the bed of the river, where the feet of the priests that bore the ark stood firm (Joshua 4:3). They were to be a reminder, to generations yet unborn, that the ark had stood still in the midst of the place of death, that the people might pass clean over into the place of life.

The type speaks eloquently to us of the condition in which we were and of what God hath wrought for us.

"We in death were lying."

By sin came death; "and so death passed upon all men, for that all have sinned" (Romans 5:12); but Jesus, the true Ark of the Covenant, stood in our place in death, so that we might be clear of it for ever and stand with Him in resurrection life. Can we think of the way God has taken to deliver us without being profoundly moved? Love was the source of it all, and love has carried it out; love that many waters could not quench and which could not be extinguished by all the billows of death; and, if the waters of death could not put out the fervent flame of this love, neither can the ages of time dim its brightness. It is eternal and omnipotent. As we see this love shining out in such direct contrast to the hateful selfishness of the flesh, are we not delighted to know that God's gracious and all-wise plan was that we should be cut off from the flesh and be linked up with the love for ever?

But the twelve stones were placed clear out of Jordan's swelling waves; they were set up in the land of promise where Jehovah's rich blessing was the people's portion, and they are typical of the Christian's place today. We no longer stand in condemnation and death but in Christ, in the full light of God's favour, in the land of promise which flows with milk and honey. This place of blessing before God has not been obtained by any work or merit of ours. It is God who has established us in Christ, and hath anointed us, and also sealed us, and given us the earnest of His Spirit in our hearts (2 Corinthians 1:21-22). We have been accepted in the Beloved, and blessed with all spiritual blessings in heavenly places in Christ (Ephesians 1:3, 6).

Now we may not understand what all this means, but it is evidently something great and good, and it is what God *has done* for us, so that the very sound of it makes our hearts beat more quickly, and fills us with longing to enter into the joy of it all. And the more clearly we see that it is by grace that we are thus saved and not of ourselves, the greater will be our desire to understand and enjoy this place of acceptance and favour.

CIRCUMCISION

Intimately linked with the twelve stones on the banks of Jordan was the circumcision of the people; and, if the former sets forth in figure God's grace to us, the latter makes known His unsparing judgment of the flesh — "it must be cut off" — and the people who were the subjects of His gracious acts in ancient days had to bear on their bodies the mark of the condemnation of the flesh.

Now God's judgment of the flesh has no such thought as a man being punished for a crime and being restored to society after that punishment had been borne. The meaning is totally different. It is the setting aside of the flesh entirely as a means of glory to God or blessing to man. Full of meaning are the words of Jesus: "The flesh profiteth nothing" (John 6:63). It is absolutely and utterly void of good. You may be sure that this is the case or God would not have cleared the ground of it. But, let us keep in mind that He has done this that all blessing might be of Himself, and so established on an immovable and eternal foundation.

If we are still in doubt as to its unprofitable character, and its utter inability to appreciate what is of God, so as to render to Him what is His due, we have but to look at Calvary.

God's blessed Son had lived before the eyes of men; they had seen His ways and heard His words; He displayed in the midst of them the tenderness and grace of the Father; and at the end of it they spat in His face. He was buffeted, betrayed, and crucified as being utterly hateful and abhorrent to them. There and then the flesh disclosed its bitter enmity against God, and proved conclusively and for ever that there was no profit in it for God or for us. It proved itself, indeed, to be a wild vine, bringing forth no fruit. And having rejected God's Son, the great and final test, it has been rejected by God, and it can never be reinstated.

But, how good it is for us to learn that the death of Christ, which manifested the character of the flesh, also displayed the heart of God in all its love. It proved that He would not be thwarted in His intentions to bless men, and it also proved that this blessing must be alone on the ground of what He is and can do, and not at all on the ground of what we are.

"By grace are ye saved ... and that not of yourselves" (Ephesians 2:8). Here, in two sentences, is the summing up of the whole matter. *"By grace are ye saved"* is the setting up of the stones in the land; *"that not of yourselves"* is the circumcision of the flesh.

For four thousand years the flesh had its day, but all its wisdom, power, self-sufficiency, culture, and religion only proved useless and unprofitable. It cannot lift its head, and glory in the presence of the Lord. Condemnation and death are its true and proper doom.

Even Christ Himself was cut off from the life of the flesh, though death had no claim upon Him. He might have lived for ever in the condition which He assumed, for His flesh was holy; every fibre of His blessed constitution was devoted to God; He fulfilled every responsibility perfectly, and no taint of sin ever marred His perfect humanity. Had He lived on in that condition He would have lived alone: but He died, and in His death sin in the flesh was condemned.

In the death of Christ we see the complete setting aside of the flesh, for death is the end of it — it has met its judgment. Though we have not actually died, in God's reckoning we have passed off the ground of the flesh; and this is also true of faith. We do not now stand before God on the ground of what we are, for on that ground we could only be condemned, but we stand before Him in Christ and there is nothing but favour. We are *buried with Him ... quickened together with Him ... risen with Him* (Colossians 2:12-13). "Buried with Him in baptism." The mark of death is upon us, and we henceforth take the place of death to that life of flesh and sin.

Now death to the unconverted man would mean the cutting off from all that made up life to him. But I am persuaded that if we view it in the light in which God presents it to us, we shall find in it the door of liberty: for this true circumcision of Christ, "not made with hands", is *the sign of the Christian's freedom.*

THE FLESH

The flesh will always serve the law of sin, and sin is a cruel task-master, like unto the Egyptians who made Israel to serve with rigour; *and the only way of freedom from this great slave-owner is by death*. A man owns a slave and holds him in hard bondage, but there comes a day when that slave no longer answers the master's call. He is dead, and there ends the domination of the master. "But", you may say, "I am not dead; I have not received the wages that sin pays." That is true; but it is also true that Jesus, in perfect love, received them for you, that you might take your place in death with Him, and be freed from the old task-master so as to serve God; for it is your privilege to reckon the death of your Substitute as yours.

The well-known Napoleonic story will illustrate this. A citizen had been called to fight, but another had gone under his name and number, and was killed in the battle. Shortly afterwards, other men were wanted for Napoleon's wars, and again this citizen was called upon, but he claimed freedom from service on the ground that, at such and such a battle, he had died in the person of his substitute. The case was referred to the Emperor, who upheld his claim. "Likewise reckon ye also yourselves to be dead indeed unto sin, but alive unto God through Jesus Christ our Lord" (Romans 6:11). Thus will you be free to yield yourself to God, and to walk in the blessed liberty of the Spirit, and enjoy the fatness of the land into which He has brought you.

But we are anticipating that which our story unfolds. Let us again link these two things together:—

(1) The stones on the banks of Jordan set forth our place of association with Christ in the favour of God — which place is all of His grace.

(2) Circumcision means that the flesh has no place there: it could not obtain that place: nor could it stand in it, for it is utterly without merit, and most evil and offensive in God's sight. "They that are in the flesh cannot please God."

The Death of Eglon

From his musings at Gilgal Ehud returned to King Eglon, but his mission on this occasion was very different to the former one. He now carried no present from an enslaved people, but a message from a delivering God. "I have a message from God unto thee." And that message was one of judgment; for the two-edged dagger, plunged into the very heart of the king, was the judgment of God upon the one who had held Israel in bondage.

We have already seen that God has condemned the flesh once and for all, and that He will never go back upon this; for He has proved it to be without profit, and we must come to the same conclusion in our experience. We have to learn that there is no profit in the flesh for us, and so shall we be prepared to accept God's condemnation of it, and thus, truly plunge the two-edged dagger into the heart of it.

The man who had been to Gilgal could not tolerate the presence and domination of Eglon in the land and lives of the people of God; nor shall we tolerate the flesh and its workings in our lives if we have truly learnt the lessons which Gilgal teaches; instead, we shall be most unsparing in our judgment of its slightest movements.

There is much confusion in the minds of many Christians as to what judging the flesh really means. Some are always bemoaning their badness and failure, and are very miserable in consequence, and they imagine that this is self-judgment. It is the very opposite.

SELF-OCCUPATION IS NOT SELF-JUDGMENT

It is often and truly said that the devil does not care whether you are occupied in praising or scolding yourself so long as you are taken up with self. For you must know that you can never be greater or rise higher than that with which you are occupied; and as long as self fills your eyes Christ is eclipsed.

If you have said there is no good in the flesh you have said all that needs to be said, and it is now your right and privilege to turn from it to Him who is altogether and for ever good, and be occupied with Him. Paul had plunged the knife into the flesh when he wrote: *"We are the circumcision, which* worship God in the Spirit, and rejoice in Christ Jesus, and *have no confidence in the flesh"* (Philippians 3:3).

When a vote of no confidence is moved and carried in the British House of Commons the Government falls and a new ministry takes it place. This is what you must do: move a vote of no confidence in the flesh. How can it be done? Cease to support it upon the government benches; turn away to the Lord, and let God's Holy Spirit have the reins and guide you henceforward. You do not trust a person in whom you have no confidence; you would not commit to such a one your secrets, much less allow him to direct and control your life; and yet, is not this the way you have treated the flesh? Thence the failure and bondage. Oh, take the two-edged sword of God's truth, as to its worthlessness, and plunge it to the hilt into the heart of it; have done with it — cast it aside — no longer be on speaking terms with it — and henceforward walk in the happy liberty of the Spirit and occupation with Christ.

Then it will be evident that you have reached God's conclusion as to the matter, and you will be true to your circumcision.

THE HAPPY RESULTS

Then Ehud went to Mount Ephraim. Ephraim means "the fruitful place", and we are able to bring forth fruit for God just in that measure in which the flesh is judged. We have been joined to Christ by the Spirit in resurrection life that we might bring forth fruit unto God, and the Spirit of God is within us in order to reproduce in us that which has come out in Jesus, so that God may be glorified through us.

It was in Ephraim that Ehud was able to blow the trumpet and rally the people to share with him the victory that he had gained, and this is the result of deliverance. If the channels are free the new life, which we have in the Spirit, will flow out for the blessing of others. Unlike the flesh, the new man has nothing for "itself alone"; it delights in sharing its joys, and proves the truth of the words, "There is that [which] scattereth, and yet increaseth" (Proverbs 11:24). Along this line you will become like the man of whom John Bunyan writes [*The Pilgrim's Progress from this world to that which is to come*, Part 2, The Sixth Stage] —

> "Though some did count him mad,
> The more he cast away, the more he had."

You may tell me that you have tried to judge the flesh, and failed over and over — that it is too strong for you; but, surely, you have forgotten that God has sent His Spirit into your heart, that He is there to displace the flesh and make room for Christ, and the whole matter now hangs on your desire. Has Christ become indispensable to you? Have you found such a portion in Him and His love that your soul cries out "He alone can satisfy!"? Ah, then in dependence on the Spirit your path shall be bright indeed.

But never lose sight of the death of Christ; let the cross of Christ be your glory, for that cross is the way of victory, even as Ehud, at the fords of Jordan, typical of the truth of our death with Christ, slew ten thousand Moabites.

AND THE LAND HAD REST FOURSCORE YEARS

There is a sweet sound about that! It is the harbour after the tossing sea; it is home after the weary conflict; it is the experience of the soul that can say: "I thank God through Jesus Christ our Lord" (Romans 7:25); and henceforth find its delight and food in Him alone.

LET US NOW FINALLY WEIGH THE ISSUES

Is there any advantage in living after the flesh? What saith the Scriptures?

> "The mind[ing] of the flesh is death" (Romans 8:6, N.Tr.).

> "He that soweth to his flesh shall of the flesh reap corruption" (Galatians 6:8). This is the present result and is unalterably the experience of all who sow to the flesh. The moment of sowing may have ministered self-gratification, but the reaping has been bondage and sorrow, regret and spiritual death.

> "For if ye live after the flesh, ye shall die" (Romans 8:13). The final end of that road.

But what is the advantage of living and walking in the Spirit?

> "The mind of the Spirit [is] life and peace" (Romans 8:6, N.Tr.).

"If ye through the Spirit do [put to death] the deeds of the body, ye shall live" (Romans 8:13).

"He that soweth to the Spirit shall of the Spirit reap life everlasting" (Galatians 6:8).

It might further help us if we put side by side "the works of the flesh" and "the fruit of the Spirit".

Works of the Flesh:	Fruit of the Spirit:
Adultery	Love
Fornication	Joy
Uncleanness	Peace
Lasciviousness	Longsuffering
Idolatry	Gentleness
Witchcraft	Goodness
Hatred	Faith
Variance	Meekness
Emulations	Temperance
Wrath	(Galatians 5:19-23).
Strife	
Sedition	
Heresies	
Envyings	"For the fruit of
Murders	the Spirit is in all
Drunkenness	goodness and right-
Revellings	eousness and truth"
and such like.	(Ephesians 5:9).

THE FINAL VICTORY

But the time is coming when the flesh shall no more hold sway, for *"There shall come a Star out of Jacob, and a Sceptre shall rise out of Israel, and shall smite the corner [or pillars] of Moab"* (Numbers 24:17). In prophetic vision even the false Balaam beheld the ascendency of the coming Christ over Moab. He was to rise as the star of hope for His enslaved people. He was to take the sceptre, and, ruling them in righteousness, deliver them for ever from their oppressors. What is not yet true for Israel must now be true for you. Christ Jesus must be our pole-star, our light, our hope, our guide, and He must sway the sceptre in your life. Oh, let it be so! Enthrone Him in your hearts: crown Him with your undivided affection: let Him be supreme.

"Crown Him Lord of all!"

HOW TO OVERCOME

Canaanites: Type of The Devil

"And the children of Israel again did evil in the sight of the LORD, when Ehud was dead. And the LORD sold them into the hand of Jabin, king of Canaan, that reigned in Hazor; the captain of whose host was Sisera, which dwelt in Harosheth of the Gentiles. And the children of Israel cried unto the LORD: for he had nine hundred chariots of iron; and twenty years he mightily oppressed the children of Israel.

"And Deborah, a prophetess, the wife of Lapidoth, she judged Israel at that time. And she dwelt under the palm tree of Deborah between Ramah and Bethel in mount Ephraim: and the children of Israel came up to her for judgment. And she sent and called Barak the son of Abinoam out of Kedesh-naphtali, and said unto him, Hath not the LORD God of Israel commanded, saying, Go and draw toward mount Tabor, and take with thee ten thousand men of the children of Naphtali and of the children of Zebulun? And I will draw unto thee to the river Kishon Sisera, the captain of Jabin's army, with his chariots and his multitude; and I will deliver him into thine hand. And Barak said unto her, If thou wilt go with me, then I will go: but if thou wilt not go with me, then I will not go. And she said, I will surely go with thee: notwithstanding the journey that thou takest shall not be for thine honour; for the LORD shall sell Sisera into the hand of a woman. And Deborah arose, and went with Barak to Kedesh.

THE DEVIL

"And Barak called Zebulun and Naphtali to Kedesh; and he went up with ten thousand men at his feet: and Deborah went up with him. Now Heber the Kenite, which was of the children of Hobab the father in law of Moses, had severed himself from the Kenites, and pitched his tent unto the plain of Zaanaim, which is by Kedesh. And they showed Sisera that Barak the son of Abinoam was gone up to mount Tabor. And Sisera gathered together all his chariots, even nine hundred chariots of iron, and all the people that were with him, from Harosheth of the Gentiles unto the river of Kishon. And Deborah said unto Barak, Up; for this is the day in which the Lord hath delivered Sisera into thine hand: is not the Lord gone out before thee? So Barak went down from mount Tabor, and ten thousand men after him. And the Lord discomfited Sisera, and all his chariots, and all his host, with the edge of the sword before Barak; so that Sisera lighted down off his chariot and fled away on his feet. But Barak pursued after the chariots, and after the host, unto Harosheth of the Gentiles: and all the host of Sisera fell upon the edge of the sword; and there was not a man left."

JUDGES 4:1-16

HOW TO OVERCOME

Chapter 4
How to Overcome the Devil

The Canaanites, with Sisera as the captain of their hosts, are figurative of the devil and his power, and we shall see in the victory of Deborah and Barak the way in which the devil has been, and still may be, a defeated foe.

There are several features in the story which prove that we have the devil's domination and defeat before us.

(1) Sisera was the great leader, and his name means, "he that binds with chains", and we are well aware that the great captive-maker is Satan himself. He was finally destroyed by that which was very weak in itself — his head was bruised, even to death, by a woman and a nail of the tent, and JESUS, the woman's Seed, has bruised the serpent's head. Men despised Him, because He was meek and lowly; His death was weakness and folly in their eyes, but —

> *"By that which seemed defeat,*
> *He won the meed and crown,*
> *Trod all our foes beneath His feet,*
> *By being trodden down."*

(2) It was a woman who raised the song of thanksgiving at Sisera's overthrow, and this links our story with the defeat of Pharaoh at the Red Sea, and of Goliath in the valley of Elah. Each of these incidents sets forth a different phase of the Lord's victory over Satan, but they all have this one striking feature — the women appreciate the greatness of the triumph. At the defeat of Pharaoh "Miriam … took a timbrel in her hand; and all the women went out after her with timbrels and with dances. And Miriam answered them, Sing ye to the LORD, for He hath triumphed gloriously" (Exodus 15:20-21). At the overthrow of Goliath "the women answered one another as they played, and said … David [has slain] his ten thousands" (1 Samuel 18:7). And now, at the defeat of Sisera, Deborah sings: "I, even I, will sing unto the LORD; I will sing praise to the LORD God of Israel" (Judges 5:3). This sets forth the grace of God most beautifully, for the woman was the first to fall before the wiles of Satan, and the woman is typical of the Church — the Bride of Christ, which is made up of all who have believed the gospel of our salvation. None will appreciate the triumph of the Lord over death and the devil like this ransomed host and from them will rise the fullest and sweetest song of praise. The angels must rejoice at Satan's overthrow, but we, who have been deceived by his lies, and known the bitterness of his bondage, can enter most truly into the triumph of the Lord over him. We can say, "Bless ye the Lord!" For "where sin abounded, grace did much more abound" (Romans 5:20).

(3) In Deborah's song we have, for the first time in Scripture, the expression, "captivity led captive"

(Judges 5:12), which undoubtedly refers to the Lord's victory over Satan, and of which we will speak presently.

How Satan works

It will be well for us clearly to understand what Satan's real work is, and how he has succeeded in enslaving the human race. From the very outset his effort has been to blind the eyes of men to the true character of God, so that instead of loving and praising God they might hate and curse Him, and instead of walking in the highway of His will they might wander in the dark and crooked paths of their own lawless desire. And so, in the story before us, we do not get the song of praise until Sisera is overthrown; and Deborah has to confess that, throughout the twenty years of Israel's captivity to the King of Canaan, the highways were unoccupied and travellers walked in the crooked paths (chapter 5:6).

We know that man was made upright, and so long as he remained faithful to his Creator he was possessed of everything that could make his life one thrilling anthem. God beheld the work of His hand and saw that it was very good, for His noblest creature stood before Him as a well-tuned instrument of praise. But Satan succeeded in turning men from God and light and liberty and song. He looked upon that fair scene with eyes of malice, and, that he might spoil it all, lied concerning God. He maligned God's character to the woman, and thus proved his right to the title, "A liar, and the father of it" (John 8:44). His proposal was: "Break God's command, and ye shall be as gods", which meant, God is not as good as He pretends to be, listen to me, and you will do better for yourselves than God has done for you; put self first, and leave God and His will out of your reckoning. The temptation succeeded; the lie was believed; sin came in and light went out. The chord was lost, the music died out, and man, that fair instrument of praise, lay broken and spoiled in the power of the foe. It seemed as though God had met with defeat and that Satan held the field, for he made the heart of man, in which God ought to have been enshrined, his citadel, and succeeded in enlisting men in his rebellion against God; and to this day he keeps them in captivity by keeping them in darkness; for we read: "If our gospel be hid, it is hid to them that are lost: in whom the god of this world hath blinded the minds of them which believe not, lest the light of the glorious gospel of Christ, who is the image of God, should shine unto them" (2 Corinthians 4:3-4). And our Lord declared: "Those by the wayside are they that hear; then cometh the devil, and taketh away the word out of their hearts, lest they should believe and be saved" (Luke 8:12). So that we see very clearly that Satan gained his power over men at the beginning by blinding them to the truth of God's character, and he keeps them in bondage in the same way.

How Satan's power has been overthrown

But how has Satan's power been overthrown? There are three things which were prominent in connection with Sisera's defeat. First of all we have Deborah. Deborah means "activity", or, "like a bee". She was wedded to Lapidoth, which means "light"; and in Deborah's song she finds much cause for thanksgiving in the fact that the people willingly offered themselves. "When the people willingly offered themselves" (chapter 5:2). "The governors of Israel that offered themselves willingly" (chapter 5:9). "A people that jeoparded their lives unto the death" (chapter 5:18).

Here then are the three things which are essential to victory over Satan: (1) Light. (2) Activity. (3) The willing offering. These three things were seen most blessedly in the Lord Jesus Christ, and He, by them, overcame the devil completely. It is in the Gospel of John that we have the statement: "Now shall the prince of this world be cast out" (chapter 12:31); and it is in the same Gospel that we have these three things of which I have spoken made prominent:—

(1) "I am the light of the world" (chapters 8:12; 9:5).

(2) "My Father worketh hitherto, and I work" (chapter 5:17).
"I must work" (chapter 9:4).

(3) "The good shepherd giveth his life for the sheep" (chapter 10:11).
"I lay down my life" (chapter 10:17).

Darkness is ignorance of God, and, when Jesus came to earth, gross darkness covered the people. He came to declare God's true character, and to make known His heart of love. But this light was not passive; it shone forth in all the activities of God's beloved Son. Light and activity were wedded together in Him, nor can they be divorced. We see that light shining in the works and words of Jesus. He fed the multitude when it fainted with hunger. He gave relief where sorrow held sway. The sick received health, and the dead, life. He blessed the children and wept over sinners; but in all these things He was but displaying the character of God. The words and works were all His Father's, so that He could say: "He that hath seen Me hath seen the Father" (chapter 14:9). Now the light that shone forth in the activities of His grace was for the deliverance of men from the thraldom of Satan, who had held them in darkness and ignorance of God; and the shining of this light was not in vain, for some could say: "We beheld His glory, the glory as of the only begotten of the Father, full of grace and truth" (chapter 1:14). But more was needful than the display of God in His life: He had to become a willing offering, for only by His death could the prince of this world be cast out and the power of death taken out of his hand. It was only by the death of Christ that the light of God's love could reach you and me; but in that death the light of love, the activity of infinite compassion, and the offering up of the devoted sacrifice were combined.

Let us recall that notable scene. When Pilate brought Jesus forth wearing the crown of thorns and the purple robe, and, presenting Him to the multitude, exclaimed: "Behold the Man!" — the world was on its trial. Did it, in that supreme moment, return to its allegiance to its Creator, and signify such a return by bowing down in lowly submission to His Son who stood before it? Oh, no! Instead they cried: "Away with Him, crucify Him!" "Then delivered he Him therefore unto them to be crucified. And they took Jesus, and led Him away" (John 19:16). In that culminating act of rebellion we see how Satan dominated men. They were so completely under his yoke that, there and then, they attempted the murder of One who was their God.

I am firmly of the opinion that if the Lord had used His power, and destroyed that devil-deceived and rebellious multitude by the breath of His mouth, Satan's object would have been gained; for then would men have remained in ignorance for ever as to God's love, and sin would have proved greater than God's grace. All the powers of darkness were marshalled against the Lord, and men were so blinded and driven by those same powers that nothing would still their frenzy but His blood. Did the devil hope that that would be the unpardonable sin? and that in pouring out his own inveterate hatred against the Son of God he was involving the whole race of men in his own irretrievable and eternal ruin? How complete then has been his defeat, for instead of Jesus manifesting His glory as the Judge of all, we read, that, "He bearing His cross went forth into a place called the place of a skull, which is called in the Hebrew Golgotha" (chapter 19:17). He went forth that the blood which sinful men were determined to shed might be efficacious for their redemption.

"They led Him away": in that their guilt reached its flood tide. "He went forth": in this was manifested the great victory of divine love over human hate. He was not dragged forth, nor driven forth: He went forth. No man took His life from Him: He laid it down Himself. The shouts of the rabble smote His ear, and, with a holy sensitiveness, He keenly felt it all, and yet no thought of saving Himself was in His heart. In majestic lowliness He went forth, bearing His cross, to accomplish that for which He came.

He knew, to its last bitterness, all that the cross meant. He was not taken by surprise, nor did He go forth on the impulse of a moment. On the night that was passed in Gethsemane's garden He had looked into the darkness and had fully counted the cost. He had talked of it on the holy mount with Moses and Elias. This hour had been planned in the council chamber of Eternity ere ever He came, and He could not draw back. There was no resistance, no regret, and every step He took towards Golgotha, shook the kingdom of the devil. And "there they crucified Him"; and the crucified Christ is God's answer to the devil's lies in Eden. "For God so loved the world, that He gave His only begotten Son, that whosoever believeth in Him should not perish, but have everlasting life" (John

3:16). If God had left us to reap the bitter harvest of our rebellion and sin, we could not have complained; but, instead of this, He undertook to dispel the darkness and overthrow the power of the devil, by this mighty and convincing proof of His love for us. Satan had made men believe that God was a hard master, gathering where He had not strawed. God has proved that He is full of love by giving the very best gift that heaven contained, even His own beloved Son, to bear the penalty of our sin, and it is when the glorious light of this love shines into the hearts of men that Satan's thraldom comes to an end. Jesus was lifted up upon the cross, and that lifting up has declared the whole truth, and we who believe it have been drawn to Him. He has become our great attractive centre, and the devil no longer holds us as his prey. The lie is laid bare, the darkness of ignorance past, and God has triumphed; for the prince of this world is cast out of the hearts of those who believe. He no longer holds them as his citadel. They have surrendered themselves to the God whose perfect love has been demonstrated in the cross of Christ.

How great is the splendour of Calvary! By its glorious light we have been awakened from our night sleep as by the rising sun at morn. We have been compelled to exclaim: "Then God did love us, after all!" The entrance of His word has given light, and with light has come liberty. The curtains of darkness have been torn asunder, and our souls have stepped forth into the day.

Science has revealed to us the fact that light, like sound, is caused by vibrations, and with all vibration there is music, and if the auditory nerve were as sensitive as the optical we should hear the music of the light as well as see its beauty. Certainly the light of God's love brings sweetest melody with it — even the melody of heaven — and the chord that was lost in Eden is found again; only the music is sweeter, the strain higher, and the glory of the praise more wonderful. As we gaze upon Him, who is now upon the throne, and in whose face all the brightness of God's grace shines, our hearts are kept in tune, and our whole souls vibrate in responsive praise to the love of God.

Nor have we any doubt as to the completeness of the triumph of Jesus, for He is alive from the dead, and His glorious words to us are: "Fear not; I am the first and the last: I am He that liveth, and was dead; and, behold, I am alive for evermore, Amen; and have the keys of hell and of death" (Revelation 1:17-18).

Since the Lord has gained so signal a victory over Satan, it is the privilege of those who have been delivered from his power to overcome as well — to be "more than conquerors, through Him that loved us" (Romans 8:37). And if we turn again to the overthrow of Sisera we shall be helped in seeing how this can come about.

BARAK WAS CALLED FROM KEDESH

He dwelt at Kedesh, which means, "sanctuary — the place of refuge". It was, in fact, the first-named of the cities of refuge which were set apart for the manslayers in Israel, and in which such dwelt securely (Joshua 20:7, 9). Whether Barak had been compelled to seek refuge there from the avenger of blood or not we cannot say; but it is certainly true that it is from the position typified in Kedesh that we go forth to the conflict with the foe. Christ is the true and great antitype of Kedesh. Death was the penalty due to our sins, and we were held in bondage by the terror of it, but we have fled for refuge to the only hope of death-doomed sinners — the Lord Jesus Christ. In Him we have salvation and a perfect deliverance from the fear of death. The devil can no longer hold us in abject bondage by the thought of it, for Jesus died to "deliver them who through fear of death were all their lifetime subject to bondage" (Hebrews 2:15). And, being safe in Christ — dwelling in the true Kedesh — we can face the enemy boldly, and take up the song of triumph: "O death, where is thy sting? O grave, where is thy victory?" (1 Corinthians 15:55).

But our great foe is full of wiles. The activities of Satan are tireless, and many an ambush will he lay in which to ensnare us; and, if we are to be overcomers, we shall need to be sober, vigilant, and watchful.

How we overcome

There are those who imagine that the Christian pathway is one of ease; that, since the future is all secured for them, all must be peace for ever, and that they may dream themselves into heaven without trouble or exercise. How mistaken are such. We have peace with God, and may always have peace as to our circumstances, but there must be no peace with the foe. We are exhorted to —

"Be strong in the Lord …"

"Put on the whole armour of God …"

"Stand against the wiles of the devil."

"Wrestle against … principalities and powers."

"Give no place to the devil."

"Resist the devil and he will flee from you."

"Whom resist, steadfast in the faith."

This is not the language of the couch of down, but of the battle-field, and we need to be fully equipped if we are to be overcomers in the fight.

You will remember that three things have already been made prominent in Sisera's overthrow, namely: Light, Activity, and the Willing Sacrifice. These three things, so perfectly displayed in the Lord, will need to be reproduced in us if we are to become overcomers.

(1) WE OVERCOME THE DEVIL BY THE WORD OF GOD

Our text for the first shall be: "I have written unto you, young men, because ye are strong, and the word of God abideth in you, and ye have overcome the wicked one" (1 John 2:14). This is light, for the Scripture saith: "The entrance of Thy words giveth light" (Psalm 119:130). The young men in the Christian sense of the word know God in His true character. This light is in them, and they are fortified and made strong by it, and the devil cannot shift them from their position. They are enabled, moreover, by the word of God, to overcome him — to make him flee from them. The devil can only overcome by darkness and lies, but these must fly away before the light and the truth.

The Scriptures must be our constant study, and so shall we be able to build ourselves up in our most holy faith: then the truth of God will be our shield and buckler. It was by the word of God that Jesus overcame the devil, and as God's word is hid in our hearts, so shall we have it ever ready to meet the foe.

Thousands who have really trusted in the Saviour are still greatly harassed by the devil, and are kept in constant doubt and fear, because the full light of the gospel is not theirs. If it were, his attacks would be in vain. When the devil brought the long catalogue of Luther's sins before him, in the hope of overcoming and affrighting him, his reply was: "The blood of Jesus Christ, His Son, cleanseth me from all sin." And with that blessed truth abiding in him he was able to overcome the devil.

But there are others, who, in times of stress and trial are attacked by the enemy in another way. He would tempt them to doubt the love of God towards them. "How can God love me and permit me to be in such trying circumstances?" is the question in many hearts. A Christian of our acquaintance, who was thus tempted, exclaimed: "Though He slay me I will trust Him!" and the devil was put to flight. But, if all Christians who are tempted, truly believed that they are loved by an unchanging and almighty love, would they give way to the temptation and allow doubts and murmurings and complaints a place in their lives? No, for their hearts would be garrisoned by the knowledge that, if God loves them perfectly, that which He permits must be the best for them, and so Satan would have no power to make them doubt the God whom they know.

We must remember that Satan gains the victory when he makes us doubt God. It was thus that he triumphed in Eden; it is thus he triumphs still; and only as the truth of God abides in us are we strong to resist his attacks.

(2) WE OVERCOME THE DEVIL BY THE ACTIVITIES OF DIVINE GRACE

It would be wrong for us to sit at ease, and, being blessed ourselves, to eat our morsel alone. To do so would be undoubted proof of our complete failure to be what God would have us, and thus also prove that Satan had gained an advantage over us; for Satan triumphs if we falsify the character of God, which we are here to display.

"As My Father hath sent Me, even so send I you" (John 20:21), are wonderful words for us to listen to, and set the high standard for our life down here. It is God's intention that we should be kept in the activities of His grace, showing forth His character in that corner in which He has put us.

I know that some people are very fond of harking back to Luke 10:38-42, and putting Mary, sitting at Jesus' feet, in contrast to Martha, who busied herself in service; but the story is often set in the wrong light, and the interpretation is in consequence very much fogged. Let us go back and consider the Lord's words that precede this incident. In verse 37, there are two words which we will put in capitals — they are, "GO" and" DO". You could not find two smaller words than these in the English language, but it would be impossible to find any more forceful and vigorous. They pulsate with life; they vibrate with energy; and they are the command of Jesus. But, He adds "likewise", and as the meaning of that qualification forces itself home, we see at once the necessity of sitting at His feet. How can we go and do like Him unless we learn of Him? It was here that Martha failed. She had got the words "go" and "do", but she forgot the qualifying word "likewise", and as a consequence her service was marred by worry and trouble, and she served in a cross and carping spirit. Mary's place at Jesus' feet must indeed be ours. It must always be the attitude of our souls. But be assured that those who sit there will most truly and constantly be found in the activities of the grace of God.

This grace must first show itself in the innermost circle, amongst our fellow Christians. If we fail here we shall be terribly crippled in the wider circle of the world: and that the devil is anxious to trip us in this inner circle is evident from Paul's second letter to the Corinthians. There was in that church a brother who had grievously sinned, but repentance had done its work, and he was full of sorrow and longed to be restored to the comfort and fellowship of God's people. But they evidently kept him at arm's length, and were not ready to forgive him. The keen-sighted apostle sees in this reluctance of theirs a wile of the devil, and he writes earnestly to them to let grace flow out, or Satan would get an advantage. Had they done other than that urged by Paul they would have failed to display God's character, and the repentant brother would have been swallowed up with sorrow, and Satan would have triumphed over both.

It had evidently forced itself upon Peter that this was the spirit in which the Lord intended that His disciples should act when He said: "Lord, how oft shall my brother sin against me, and I forgive him? till seven times? Jesus saith unto him, I say not unto thee, Until seven times: but, Until seventy times seven" (Matthew 18:21-22). There must be no limit to the activities of grace in this circle. We must not be weary in well-doing, but ever keep in mind that word "likewise".

Let us awake to the fact that harshness and legality in our dealings one with the other spells victory for Satan. Let us also keep in mind that gentleness, forbearance and love are for the glory of God.

But these activities also manifest themselves in seeking the good of souls. When Christ ascended on high He fulfilled the prophetic song of Deborah and led captivity captive. From that place of power He has bestowed gifts upon men, for the edifying and building up of His own people, so that in spite of all the enemy's attempts to throw them down, and his *cunning craftiness*, they might not be deceived by him or turned away from the truth (Ephesians 4:9-14). It is within the reach of all who are near the Lord to carry sweet thoughts of Christ about to others, with the result that joy takes the place of depression in the hearts of those who hear, and the temptations of Satan thus lose their power.

God's grace to the world

It is our privilege also to tread in the steps of Jesus, our Lord and Pattern, and carry to those who have fallen beneath the power of the devil that which can completely deliver them. "Shall the prey be taken from the mighty, or the lawful captive delivered?" was asked long ago (Isaiah 49:24). We have the answer to that question today, for the gospel concerning God's Son has delivering power, and *every soul saved is a fresh bit of territory wrenched from Satan's domination — a fresh bit of territory added to the Lord's kingdom.* How glorious to see the dark flag hauled down and the devil driven out; to see the Lord come in and take possession and use that new bit of territory as a vantage point from which fresh victories may be gained.

This is the Lord's own work, but He is pleased to put it into the hands of those whom He has delivered, for we read:

> "How shall they hear without a preacher?" (Romans 10:14).
> "They … so spake, that a great multitude … believed" (Acts 14:1).
> "He which converteth the sinner from the error of his way shall save a soul from death, and shall hide a multitude of sins" (James 5:20).

But the conflict is real and fierce, and foot by foot the devil will contend for the ground that he holds. We must realize that we are confronted by his power, then shall we turn away from any fancied wisdom and strength of our own to the Lord alone. We shall desire earnestly to carry out the glad tidings, but we shall seek constantly the place where true power and wisdom are to be found — even the presence of the Lord — and so shall we prove that dependence on Him alone is the way of victory.

"Finally, my brethren, be strong in the Lord, and in the power of His might. Put on the whole armour of God, that ye may be able to stand against the wiles of the devil. For we wrestle not against flesh and blood, but against principalities, against powers, against the rulers of the darkness of this world, against spiritual wickedness in high places. Wherefore, take unto you the whole armour of God, that ye may be able to withstand in the evil day, and having done all to stand. Stand therefore, having your loins girt about with truth, and having on the breastplate of righteousness; and *your feet shod with the preparation of the gospel of peace*; above all, taking the shield of faith, wherewith ye shall be able to quench all the fiery darts of the wicked [one]. And take the helmet of salvation, and the sword of the Spirit, which is the word of God: praying always with all prayer and supplication in the Spirit, and watching thereunto with all perseverance and supplication for all saints; *and for me, that utterance may be given unto me*, that I may open my mouth boldly, to make known the *mystery of the gospel*" (Ephesians 6:10-19).

The gospel of the grace of God makes way for that which is behind it, and with this end in view, Christians are exhorted to wrestle and pray; for the ultimate result of the preaching of the gospel is the triumph of what God is in His nature and activities, and the utter confounding of the enemy.

"Curse ye Meroz." Are any who profess Christianity indifferent as to this conflict? Let them hear the solemn words: "Curse ye Meroz, said the angel of the LORD, curse ye bitterly the inhabitants thereof; because they came not to the help of the LORD, to the help of the LORD against the mighty" (Judges 5:23). Oh! why did Reuben abide by the sheep-fold while the great conflict raged? Why, oh, why do Christians today, loving ease and comfort, abide in the safety of the sheep-folds, when God's glorious gospel is going forth, and is opposed by all the power and ingenuity of Satan? Surely where such indifference holds sway the devices of Satan have been successful, and he has got an advantage. The Lord grant us grace so that we may forget ourselves, and go forth to the conflict, led by the light of the knowledge of Himself and the activities of His grace, until the morning dawns, when all His enemies shall perish, and when those that love Him shall be as the sun when he goeth forth in his might (Judges 5:31).

(3) We overcome Satan by being ready to sacrifice ourselves

Now, if the devil fails to make us doubt the love and goodness of God, and to hinder us from seeking the good of others, he will endeavour to overcome us by making us think much of ourselves — putting self first instead of God. This was the first evidence of departure from God in Eden. Eve thought of herself, and when she put forth her hand to take the fruit of the tree, she proved that she had begun to love SELF rather than God, and this has always been natural to men since that sad day. It was this that Satan cast in God's face when he said in the presence of the Almighty: "Skin for skin, yea, all that man hath will he give for his life. But put forth Thine hand now, and touch his bone and his flesh, and he will curse Thee to Thy face" (Job 2:4-5). Satan understood well the character of the fall. He knew that men were utterly selfish; that they would sacrifice everything, even their God, to save themselves.

In the Lord Jesus Christ, our Pattern and our Guide, we have a perfect example. He willingly sacrificed everything, even His life. When tempted by Satan to pity Himself and refuse the cross, He maintained His blessed pathway of perfect devotion to God. He loved the Lord, His God, with all his heart, His soul, His strength; and His perfect answer to the great temptation was: "The cup which My Father hath given Me, shall I not drink it?" (John 18:11).

The saints of God have the victory through Him, and Satan will be bruised beneath their feet. We have the character of this victory made plain in Revelation 12:10-11: "And I heard a loud voice saying in heaven, Now is come salvation, and strength, and the kingdom of our God, and the power of His Christ: for the accuser of our brethren is cast down, which accused them before our God day and night. And they overcame him by the blood of the Lamb, and by the word of their testimony; and *they loved not their lives unto the death.*" Here, indeed, is victory over Satan, for here are those who, in spite of all his subtlety and temptations, loved God better than themselves, and willingly laid down their lives for His testimony. God was more to them than life itself. This is God's triumph over Satan in the hearts of His people. They love God: but this is the result of His love to them, as manifested in the blood of the Lamb. That blood is the undeniable token to us of a love that would overcome every opposing force; a love that could not be quenched by the many waters of death. And this love so triumphs over them and takes captive their hearts, that it, and the truth of the God whose love it is, becomes everything to them — all else is of no account. Thus it was with the martyrs, who sang their songs of triumph amid the flames at the stake. Thus it will ever be where the love of God holds sway.

But, how do we stand in this matter? In these days we are not called upon to go to actual martyrdom for Christ's sake, yet it is our privilege every day to prove that we love Him better than ourselves. Is not this the secret of true discipleship? Do we not find it set forth in the Lord's words? "If any man come to Me, and hate not his father, and mother, and wife, and children, and brethren, and sisters, yea, and his own life also, he cannot be My disciple. And whosoever doth not bear his cross, and come after Me, cannot be My disciple" (Luke 14:26-27).

"Whosoever will come after Me, let him deny himself, and take up his cross, and follow Me. For whosoever will save his life shall lose it; but whosoever shall lose his life for My sake and the gospel's, the same shall save it" (Mark 8:34-35). There is here not self-denial, but the complete denial of self — the constant sacrificing of self, if you will, for bearing the cross means this; and in so doing — in losing our lives thus — we tread in the footsteps of the One who was ever victorious, for He —

> "*Trod all His foes beneath His feet*
> *By being trodden down."*

As we tread this path we are more than conquerors through Him. "What is it to be more than a conqueror?" was the question asked. "To kill six men and be ready to kill a seventh", was the reply given. But, was this the right answer? Ah, no! but exactly the reverse. *It is to be killed six times ourselves and be ready then to be killed again.* "For Thy sake we are killed [not killing] all the day long" (Romans 8:36). When we are thus prepared to sacrifice ourselves for His sake, we have the victory, and God is glorified in us.

But see what precedes and follows the verse quoted, and you will then understand the secret of this victory, and see how it is possible for us, who are by nature always self-centred, to rejoice in suffering. "Who shall separate us from the love of Christ? Shall tribulation, or distress, or persecution, or famine, or nakedness, ... or sword?" (verse 35). None of these physical sufferings can separate us from His love, though oft-times our souls may lose the sense of it. Then we get downcast and prone to murmur in the midst of trial: and thus Satan gains an advantage. But, if our hearts are right, and we are dependent upon the Lord, our great Intercessor, the tribulation does but drive us closer to Him, and we are thus made to prove afresh the blessedness of that love which is greater than the greatest trial. Then can we glory in tribulation: then do the dews of sorrow shine like unto precious gems, and we are content and happy with God's way for us, and are true overcomers. Then follows the blessed conclusion: "For I am persuaded, that neither death, nor life, nor angels, nor principalities, nor powers, nor things present, nor things to come, nor height, nor depth, nor any other creature, shall be able to separate us from the love of God, which is in Christ Jesus our Lord" (verses 38-39). If the first list are physical trials in which we need the love of Christ as our support, here are spiritual foes, and against these God Himself is opposed. They cannot separate us from His love, for His love is greater and mightier than them all. All the power of these spiritual things was marshalled to separate us from the love of God and to hold us in bondage, but the cross of Christ destroyed their dominion, and through His precious death, the love of God has secured us in spite of them all, and since this is a glorious fact we need not fear. Oh, may the light of this matchless love so fill and move our hearts that we may be always ready to be killed all the day long for Jesus' sake, and so be more than conquerors through Him that loved us.

Midian:
Type of Earthly Things

"And the children of Israel did evil in the sight of the LORD: and the LORD delivered them into the hand of Midian seven years. And the hand of Midian prevailed against Israel: and because of the Midianites the children of Israel made them the dens which are in the mountains, and caves and strong holds. And so it was, when Israel had sown, that the Midianites came up, and the Amalekites, and the children of the east, even they came up against them; and they encamped against them, and destroyed the increase of the earth, till thou come unto Gaza, and left no sustenance for Israel, neither sheep, nor ox, nor ass. For they came up with their cattle and their tents, and they came as grasshoppers for multitude; for both they and their camels were without number: and they entered into the land to destroy it. And Israel was greatly impoverished because of the Midianites; and the children of Israel cried unto the LORD.

"And it came to pass, when the children of Israel cried unto the LORD because of the Midianites, that the LORD sent a prophet unto the children of Israel, which said unto them, Thus saith the LORD God of Israel, I brought you up from Egypt, and brought you forth out of the house of bondage; and I delivered you out of the hand of the Egyptians, and out of the hand of all that oppressed you, and drave them out from before you, and gave you their land; and I said unto you, I am the LORD your God; fear not the gods of the Amorites, in whose land ye dwell: but ye have not obeyed my voice.

"And there came an angel of the L ord, and sat under an oak which was in Ophrah, that pertained unto Joash the Abiezrite: and his son Gideon threshed wheat by the winepress, to hide it from the Midianites. And the angel of the L ord appeared unto him, and said unto him, The L ord is with thee, thou mighty man of valour. And Gideon said unto him, Oh my Lord, if the L ord be with us, why then is all this befallen us? and where be all his miracles which our fathers told us of, saying, Did not the L ord bring us up from Egypt? but now the L ord hath forsaken us, and delivered us into the hands of the Midianites. And the L ord looked upon him, and said, Go in this thy might, and thou shalt save Israel from the hand of the Midianites: have not I sent thee? And he said unto him, Oh my Lord, wherewith shall I save Israel? behold, my family is poor in Manasseh, and I am the least in my father's house. And the L ord said unto him, Surely I will be with thee, and thou shalt smite the Midianites as one man."

Judges 6:1-16

HOW TO OVERCOME

Chapter 5
How to Overcome
Earthly Things

The Midianites are a striking figure of earthly things. They robbed the Israelites of the enjoyment of their God-given inheritance and made their lives a burden and a misery, and this is precisely what earthly things do for the Christian, when he is dominated by them.

Now the things of earth are not necessarily bad and grossly sinful. They are things which may be right and proper when kept in their right place, and they may include God's temporal mercies to us: but if they become our object in life they crowd out the things of Christ and heaven, and as a consequence the sunshine departs from the life and the song from the lips, and soul prosperity is at an end.

Briefly summed up earthly things represent the "cares", "riches", "pleasures", and "necessities" of this life. They embrace the sweet and bitter, the joy and sorrow, the prosperity and adversity of our existence here, and are found in the family, social, and business circles, and if the mind becomes absorbed with them, the seed of the Word is choked in the heart and does not bring forth fruit. This is evident from the Lord's own words, "And that which fell among thorns are they, which, when they have heard, go forth, and are choked with *cares* and *riches* and *pleasures of this life*, and bring no fruit to perfection" (Luke 8:14). "Take no thought [anxious care] for your life, what ye shall eat; ... or what ye shall drink, neither be ye of doubtful mind [live not in careful suspense]. ... But rather seek ye the kingdom of God; and all these things shall be added unto you" (Luke 12:22, 29, 31).

Those who know not God, and whose vision is bounded by the present — the nations of the world — seek after these earthly things (Luke 12:30). But as the eagle spreads his broad pinions, and soars above the earth, and bathes himself in the fair sunlight, so has the Christian received title and power to rise above the things of earth to enjoy the bright treasures of that place where Christ is pre-eminent. If, instead of fulfilling this high calling of God, he is found burrowing in the earth, there is neither fruit for God nor light for others, for these two things are intimately linked together by the Lord (Luke 8:15-16).

Earthly things are set in contrast to things in heaven, and there is a constant rivalry between them. The things in heaven belong to the Christian, but the things of earth claim his attention and would exclude from heart and mind that which is his true portion; hence the need for the exhortation, "If ye then be risen with Christ ... set your affection on *things above*, not on *things on the earth*" (Colossians 3:1-2). The condition of those who mind earthly things is most serious, even though they are Christians, for the Apostle had to write, "For many walk, of whom I have told you often, and now tell you even weeping, that they are the enemies of the cross of Christ: ... who mind *earthly things*. For our *conversation* [or citizenship] *is in heaven*" (Philippians 3:18-20).

How the Midianites treated Israel

"And they encamped against them … and left no sustenance for Israel, … and Israel was greatly impoverished because of the Midianites" (Judges 6:4, 6).

The Midianites prevailed against Israel: and because of the Midianites the children of Israel made them the dens which are in the mountains, and caves, and strongholds (Judges 6:2). In short, they hid themselves in the earth. God had set them in that land to be a witness for Himself, and if they had walked in His ways their light would have been kept brightly shining, and other nations would have learnt how good it was to have Israel's God. But they were no witness for God when hidden in the dens and caves of the earth; nor is there any light for God today in those of His people whose souls are under the power of the things of earth; their light is hidden instead of being set on the candlestick so that all may see the light.

God had brought His people into that land that they might enjoy it, and they found it to be a land flowing with milk and honey — a land of joy and gladness — where the corn grew in abundance and the cattle flourished upon its verdant hills. But when the Midianites invaded the land, and made their home there, all this was lost to them, for they came up like grasshoppers, devouring every green thing, and the people of Israel were greatly impoverished, and utterly robbed of those blessings which God had given to them.

Christian, do you find yourself in a like situation? You have allowed the things of earth to occupy your thoughts and heart, and they have invaded the land in a multitude, and have crowded out the things that are brightest and best. You can look back to the time when the things of Christ and heaven were the joy and delight of your soul, but you have lost your taste for them, and the Holy Spirit has been grieved, and your soul has become greatly impoverished. You have no time now for quiet communion with the Lord, for the Midianites have come up "with their cattle and their tents, ... as grasshoppers for multitude; ... and they [have] entered into the land to destroy it" (Judges 6:5).

Oh, it is pitiful that this is the sad case of thousands of erstwhile flourishing Christians, who have been overcome, not by gross sinfulness, nor even worldliness, but by the "things of earth"! "The family, the business, the things of this life *must be attended to*", they say, and, in consequence, the things of Christ, which are their true and proper portion as God's people, are neglected, and mark well the three-fold result:

(1)   No fruit for God.

(2)   No light for others.

(3)   No sustenance for themselves.

THE FIRST STEP TO DELIVERANCE

But in their distress Israel cried unto the Lord because of the Midianites, and that cry of need was the start of better things. They were brought to acknowledge that if God did not help them there was no hope for them; and this is an immense lesson for all to learn. Nor can it be too constantly emphasized that deliverance, in its every phase, must come from God — our striving is futile. You may have made many attempts to rid yourself of the galling yoke of earthly things, but all in vain. If you have come to the end of your own resources, then you have reached the right place for blessing; for *the end of your resources is the beginning of God's, and to His there is no end.* If your soul has become impoverished let Him hear your cry. He is unchanged; it is your own ways that have brought disaster upon you, even as the Israelites were suffering for their own disobedience (Judges 6:10).

In answer to their cry of need God raised up a deliverer for them, and of him we have a most interesting and instructive description. There are several things which stand out strikingly in his character and conduct to which attention must be called:

(i) He was able to preserve to himself some of the produce of the land of which the rest of Israel had been robbed.

(ii) He was greatly troubled because of the condition of God's people.

(iii) He had low thoughts of himself.

(iv) The main incidents in his pathway to victory took place at night or in secret.

(1) Gideon is introduced to our notice whilst threshing wheat in the secret place, to hide it from the Midianites. This wheat was the true portion of the people, for it was the produce of the land which God had given them: for us it is a type of Christ. Israel had been robbed of their sustenance, but Gideon had been able to secure some, at least, from the thieves. He evidently valued that which he guarded so carefully and would not be robbed of it if he could avoid it. It was to that man the Lord could reveal Himself, and he could be called a mighty man of valour, for he had started along the pathway to final victory.

Do you appreciate Christ, and is it your habit to retire into secret, away from the stress and worry of every-day life, in order to feed upon Him and His things, which are your true portion?

Is it possible that you have to confess that you have no time for His things, and that from dawn to sundown you are fully occupied with the duties of the day? Then, indeed, you are under the galling yoke of these most tyrannical foes of your soul — earthly things.

Make time to feed upon Christ in secret. You will soon realize the good of it. The days will be brighter, the loads less heavy, your spirit less fretful, and, perhaps, that anxious look will depart from your face. In short, a new era will dawn for you if you will but turn aside to thresh the true Corn in the secret of God's presence. You will need to guard these quiet moments jealously, for these earthly things will intrude themselves into the most sacred hours, if permitted.

It was whilst Gideon threshed the corn that the Angel of the Lord appeared unto him with the soul-thrilling announcement: "The Lord is with thee, thou mighty man of valour." The one who could hold fast to what God had given could be thus addressed; the Lord was with him, and strength and courage must be his in consequence.

(2) But Gideon was not elated at the angel's salutation. He thought of the state of the land, and he expressed his heart's deep exercise as to it. The days were not as they once had been, and he felt it deeply. It seemed as though the Lord had forsaken His people, and he is greatly troubled because of it. He had wheat himself, but he was not satisfied to

have this alone and remain indifferent to the impoverished condition of God's heritage.

And the Lord looked upon him with evident satisfaction, and said: "Go in this thy might, and thou shalt save Israel from the land of the Midianites: have I not sent thee?"

The one who truly gets to God about things must feel how lean of soul are many of God's people, and how little the precious things of Christ are known and valued. Feeling this, he will not be satisfied to eat his portion alone. Ah, no! to do so would be undeniable evidence of a heart at a distance from God. We cannot separate ourselves in thought from the rest of God's flock; their poverty and their hurt is ours.

Gideon refused to separate himself from the rest of God's people, for when the angel said, "The Lord is with *thee*", Gideon replied, "If the Lord be with *us*"; and the more we appreciate Christ the more we shall love His people and long for the deliverance of every one of them from every yoke of bondage.

(3) The third feature in Gideon's character was low thoughts of himself. He does not vaunt himself because of the way that he is addressed, but speaks instead of the poverty of his family, and of his own littleness; and this marked him still more decidedly as a chosen vessel unto the Lord; so that that which had already been announced can now be emphasized: "Thou shalt smite the Midianites as one man."

Three things always go together, and are each a distinctive mark of the grace of God in His people. (1) Appreciation of Christ; (2) Love and care for His people; (3) Low thoughts of self.

God must have His rights

Gideon was still in much ignorance as to who conversed with him, but it is pleasing to see that when the right moment came, he could bring forth the unleavened cakes, the fine flour, and a kid of the goats. The Lord accepted his offering, and said unto him: "Peace be unto thee; fear not: thou shalt not die." With increasing light there was increasing faith and vigour on Gideon's part, for he built an altar unto the Lord and called it "Jehovah-shalom", which means, "The Lord send peace". He took his stand upon God's own gracious words to himself, and claimed peace for all.

The building of that altar meant that God should have His rights — those rights of which He had been robbed for so long a time; and it is when God has His rights that He can send peace.

This, then, was the man whom God could use for the delivering of His people, and the marks of grace and faith in him are figurative of that state which must characterize us if we are to be delivered and deliverers. The man whose soul is fed upon the things of heaven will be a worshipper of God, for his heart will be filled with the things of God; and he it is who can raise the altar with a divinely given intention to render to God what is His; nor will he yield mind and heart and time to occupation with the things of earth.

Thus far the activities and progress of Gideon had been in secret and with God; we now come to his first blow at the dominion of the enemy.

An altar to the false god, Baal, had been raised in the land, and it was in consequence of this that they were suffering under the tyranny of the Midianites. Baal is the god of the sun. The sun sets forth the influences that rule the day, and the altar of Baal in the land is typical of the things of earth having ascendancy in the hearts and minds of God's people. This altar had to go to make room for God's altar, for the two could not stand together.

In the same epistle in which we are exhorted to set our affections on things above, not on things on the earth, we read — "That in all things He might have the preeminence" (Colossians 1:18). If we are to be free from bondage and walk in liberty, Christ must be pre-eminent. O Christian! does your heart respond to this? He is truly worthy of this place, and if "in all things", then, surely, in your heart and life. If the influences of the day and the things of this life have the ascendancy with you, then the things of Christ are displaced; the false god, Baal, has raised his head in the midst of your life, and, as a consequence, you are joyless and fruitless. Oh, cast down that altar; do it at once; make Christ everything. "Little children, keep yourselves from idols" (1 John 5:21).

But, mark well, it was the man who had been in secret with God who could overthrow the altar of the false god; and you can have no power against these foes except as you have to do with God in secret.

An absolute necessity

We will now pass on to the very interesting incident recorded at the end of chapter 6:33-40. The Midianites, with their allies, the Amalekites (a figure of the flesh), came forth to fight against Gideon. This was natural, and is so today. You may be sure that, if you have drawings of heart heavenward, you will have to contend with these combined powers, for the flesh loves not the things of Christ, but finds its satisfaction in the things of the earth.

But Gideon was not afraid; he blew the trumpet of warning, and gathered the people of God together, but ere he undertook to go forth to battle, he had again to speak with God in secret. In the secret of God's presence *he desired the performance of a miracle*, and that of a very peculiar kind. A very paltry one, says the scoffing critic. A very essential one to us, if we are to be victorious, is our reply. Gideon's request was that the fleece should be saturated with that of which the earth knew nothing — "let the dew be upon the fleece only and all the earth dry." The character of the animal is known by its fleece. *Then the fleece shall represent our character* in this world; but let us remember that character is formed from inside — from what the heart and mind dwell upon. Are we prepared to say to God: "Let the dew be upon the fleece; let us be saturated, baptized, entirely characterized by that which the earth does not possess?" That is Christ, surely, and it is only as our hearts and minds feed upon Him that we shall bear the heavenly character and stand out distinctly from what is of the earth. You may tell me that such is your desire, but that all your efforts in that direction have been entirely in vain. And let me assure you that your efforts always will be fruitless. You cannot perform a miracle, and to bring that about of which we speak is impossible except by the power of God.

Gideon did not propose to do this thing himself, but he yielded the fleece to God and asked Him to bring it about. And this is the secret: "Yield yourselves unto God" (Romans 6:13), and you will prove that what is impossible with men is possible with God. It is His delight, in perfect grace and by the power of the Spirit, so to fill our hearts and minds with Christ that we may bear His character in a world which knows nothing about Him. But Gideon did more than yield the fleece to God; he also displayed energy and desire in connection with this matter, for he rose early on the morrow to see the answer of God to his prayer.

God grant that we may show the same energy in our spiritual desires. We are oftentimes — alas! too often — satisfied with longing and praying, both right, but we must go further; there must be the surrender of ourselves to God; there is no substitute for this; and then the earnest seeking and waiting for the result.

Gideon had one more request to make before he took the field; it was that the fleece might be dry and all the earth wet. Here we have the negative side of the matter, which naturally follows the positive. It shall mean for us: Let us be free in heart and character from that with which the earth is saturated; let its maxims, principles, hopes and aspirations have no place in our lives, for these things can only mar our enjoyment of Himself. His cross has separated us from them, and we must be free from them practically if we are to represent Him aright.

It is interesting to note that it was in the threshing floor that these desires were expressed — in the place where Gideon had first met the Lord and where he had shown his appreciation of God's blessing; and we may also be sure that these desires are the true and natural outcome of feeding upon Christ in the secret of God's presence, away from the influences of the day and the intrusion of earthly things.

From this point onward Gideon went forward to victory. He had had much to do with God in secret, and in the strength and courage and wisdom gained there he was able to plan his campaign against the foe.

But there are still further lessons for us to learn ere we come to the final deliverance of the people, and these lessons do but emphasize what has already been before us.

THE TESTING OF THE PEOPLE

The people were too many; and there was the danger of their taking the credit of the victory to themselves, and falling thereby into a worse state than that in which they had been. More than two-thirds of them were cowards; their own skins were of more value to them than the fight of the Lord, and they were glad to return to their own homes. Do we shrink from exercise of soul? Do we seek ease and comfort rather than conflict, which we must have if we are to be overcomers? We may go on with meetings and services, read books and discuss doctrines, but, are our souls braced up in divine courage? If not, we are unsuited for the fight, and until our souls are truly revived we are disqualified for it.

Ten thousand yet remained, who were not cowards as were their former comrades; but the greater part of them were not such as God could use; so to them was applied a further and severer test.

"Bring them down to the water, and I will try them there", is God's command. Water is one of the greatest of God's mercies, and in this instance an abundant supply was brought within reach of the host, and by the way they treated it their fitness to be God's warriors, or otherwise, was manifested. Nine thousand seven hundred stooped down to get as much as they could, and, for the time, seemed to forget the fight. On the other hand, three hundred took just that which would meet their present necessity, and no more: the fight of the Lord controlled them, and all else was kept in abeyance.

THE TRUE USE OF GOD'S MERCIES

Here we see the true use of the mercies of God. We need food and clothing and shelter, and these are all put within our reach. How shall we treat them? If our object is to obtain as much of these things as possible we have become their servants, and are amongst those who cannot face the foe, for we have begun to mind earthly things. If on the contrary these things are used only as God's mercies to us, and we are content with such things as we have, remembering that we are here not to accumulate treasure on earth but for the testimony of the Lord, then shall we prove ourselves to be fit vessels for His service.

This commendable trait is manifested still further in the valiant three hundred, for they carried their victuals in their hands, enough for their need and no more. They were the right men for the war, who would not allow themselves to be entangled by the affairs of this life.

THE MUNITIONS OF WAR

They were a strangely equipped army as they went out to the fight; their weapons were contrary to all accepted ideas, and their tactics such as could not be learnt in the military schools; but they were men with the single eye and obedient and confident withal, and that was all they needed to be.

They were single-eyed men, and their gaze was fixed upon their leader, for his command was: "Look upon me." If they had looked upon the foe they would probably have been discouraged by the number of them; but to look upon the foe was no business of theirs, for their God-given captain claimed their attention and commanded their obedience, and while they looked on him "they stood every man in his place", and, standing each in his place, they became a compacted, undivided company.

Their weapons of warfare were strange: trumpets, pitchers, only held to be broken, and lamps. They carried no sword of tempered steel with them, but their battle cry was a glorious one, and proved that they were men assured of victory. And, indeed, they were not disappointed, for as they cried, "The sword of the LORD, and of Gideon, … the [whole] host [of Midian] ran, and cried, and fled" (chapter 7:20-21).

In Paul's second letter to Timothy we have the New Testament counterpart of this. The letter has been called a dark one, and truly there is a dark side to it, for in it there is plainly set forth the terrible departure from the truth of the professing Church: the result of first minding earthly things.

The state of things described in the third chapter of this letter could scarcely be worse, and yet we have there a true picture of the professing Church today, and it is evident that if the Church or any section of it is our hope and refuge — our place of salvation — then we are lost indeed. But Paul looked not in that direction; he looked above the scene of conflict and failure, and fixed his eye upon a risen Christ at God's right hand, and the result of this steadfast gaze was continual triumph. So that, viewed from this point, this letter is one of the brightest in the Book, for the failure of men only serves to throw into bright relief the faithfulness and stability of the Lord.

PAUL'S BATTLE-CRY

So Paul had a battle-cry just as had Gideon. He could link himself with the Lord's testimony and cry, *"The testimony of the Lord [and] of me His prisoner"* (2 Timothy 1:8); and he who had such a battle-cry could say, "I am not ashamed: for I know whom I have believed, and am persuaded that He is able to keep that which I have committed unto Him against that day" (1:12). He could also say at the end of the fight, "I have fought a good fight, I have finished my course, I have kept the faith" (4:7).

He had stood in his place, like Gideon's men, because he knew the might and the grace of his great Leader, who had crushed the foe and triumphed over death; and you may be sure that, as we remember Jesus Christ raised from the dead according to Paul's gospel, and have our eyes fixed upon Him in whom all God's intentions of blessing are secured, we too shall be able to stand, "every man in his place". Nor shall we stand with fear and dread and depression, for our hearts will be maintained by the triumph of the Lord, and as we stand thus in our place we shall sound the Christian's battle-cry with confidence.

THE TESTIMONY OF THE LORD

The testimony of the Lord is the blessed truth as to His victory, and that all the grace of God is in Christ, where no foe can spoil it. It is the proclaiming of the great fact that God has not been foiled, but that all His purposes of grace are held securely in the hand that smote the power of death. In short, it is the glorious gospel of God concerning His Son, as the risen Man, through whom all God's will is accomplished. The knowledge of this gospel makes us triumphant, nor shall we preach it with shame of face, for it is not about us but about Christ; not about the Church but about the mighty Saviour — the Son of God.

May we be truly controlled by the spirit of love and power, and of a sound mind, that we may determinedly go on with this glorious preaching. We may feel ashamed of the Church as a witness for Christ here, and ashamed of our own wretched selves, but here is something of which we need never be ashamed, for it is the very power and wisdom of God.

The Pitchers and the Lamps

The men who cried, "The sword of the LORD and of Gideon", were the men who held their light in earthen vessels, and those vessels had to be broken for the light to shine out. The shining of this light in the darkness had to accompany the battle-cry, and the blowing of the trumpets. Allusion is made to this in 2 Corinthians 4:7. Believers possess a wonderful treasure; it is the knowledge of God in their hearts. This glorious light is shining in all its perfection from the face of Jesus Christ, and it has shined in our hearts; but if it has shone in, it is in order that it might shine out again. The light must not be hidden; it must shine forth from the earthen vessels that hold it. This can only be in the power of God: human effort is entirely vain.

The light shone in Paul; his manner of life was in keeping with the testimony which he bore, so that if he preached that all blessing was in Christ in glory he did not look for it on earth. He looked not at the things which are seen, but at the things which are not seen. Eternal, not temporal things, commanded his soul, and thus was he a victor indeed — delivered himself and able to deliver others also.

The shining of the light and the going forth of the testimony must go together. To this the Lord has called us, and it is our privilege to connect ourselves with the name and testimony of the Lord. But let us bear in mind that if we are occupied with earthly things the light will be obscured, and we shall cease to care for the testimony of the Lord.

Here are the things that led to the overthrow of these foes by Gideon's army.

(1) They were courageous men (chapter 7:3).
(2) They took only of such things as they needed (verse 6).
(3) They were obedient to the commander (verse 17).
(4) They let the light which the pitchers contained shine out (verse 20).
(5) They shouted the battle-cry (verse 20).
(6) "They stood every man in his place" (verse 21).

God grant that the blessed antitype of these things may mark every one of us.

A WARNING

There is much more in Gideon's history that is of deepest interest and instruction which does not come within the scope of our talk: of one thing, however, we need to be warned.

The Israelites would have made Gideon their king: they speak of him as their deliverer, and seem utterly to fail to own all as from God (chapter 8:22). History repeats itself, for the hearts of men are the same, and in the Church many have fallen into this snare. Men have been raised up of God to help and deliver His people, and many have admired and followed them, and even gone so far as to call themselves by the name of the vessel whom God has used, thus making him a king over them. Against this we are warned in 1 Corinthians 1 and 3, and there is more need for the warning today than ever; for, instead of looking and cleaving to the Lord alone, the bulk of Christians are looking here and there for someone whom they may call the man of God for the time, from whom they may get guidance and light. Gideon stood true in this test and said, *"The Lord shall rule over you."*

The men of Shechem did not heed the wise words of Gideon, for at his death they made his son Abimelech, their king, with the result that he destroyed them, and they destroyed him.

The ninth chapter of Judges records for us the bitter harvest of his pride and their folly, and teaches us to beware of trusting in man — the bramble of Jotham's parable (Judges 9) — and especially so when it is a question of God's things.

The Lord alone is our sufficiency. His love and grace and power can never fail. He is the true Vine, the Olive and the Fig Tree of which Jotham spoke in contrast to the useless bramble. Yea, all His people's need is found in Him.

> *"May we with HIM be satisfied,*
> *And triumph in His Name."*

The Philistines:
Type of Carnal Religion

"And the children of Israel did evil again in the sight of the LORD; and the LORD delivered them into the hand of the Philistines forty years.

"And there was a certain man of Zorah, of the family of the Danites, whose name was Manoah; and his wife was barren, and bare not. And the angel of the LORD appeared unto the woman, and said unto her, Behold now, thou art barren, and bearest not: but thou shalt conceive, and bear a son. Now therefore beware, I pray thee, and drink not wine nor strong drink, and eat not any unclean thing: For, lo, thou shalt conceive, and bear a son; and no razor shall come on his head: for the child shall be a Nazarite unto God from the womb: and he shall begin to deliver Israel out of the hand of the Philistines."

JUDGES 13:1-5

Chapter 6
How to Overcome Carnal Religion

Who were these Philistines that held Israel in such bondage and brought them into such misery and poverty? And what do they represent? They sprang from Egypt (Genesis 10:13-14), but though they had left Egypt behind and got into the land which God had promised to His people, they had not taken His way into it; their way had been an easy and short cut by which they escaped the Red Sea and River Jordan. These things that prefigured deliverance and blessing by the death and resurrection of Christ had no place in their history. They were in the land of God's people, but they had not travelled into it by the God-ordained way (Exodus 13:17). Really they had no right in the land at all, for God had apportioned it to Israel (Deuteronomy 32:8-9). *They are figurative of secularized Christianity, religion made acceptable to unregenerate men.* Ritualism and Modernism are some of the Philistines of our day; they are really pagan superstitions and philosophies that have invaded the sphere of faith and made it like a great house of mixed vessels (2 Timothy 2:20); and they are sorely oppressing the true Israel of God. They draw near to God with the lips, but are scornful of that heart exercise and spiritual life that have marked the revivals of former days. They claim to be children of God, but they have no title to that relationship, for they have not received God's only begotten Son by faith, and have not been born again (John 1:12-13). They have the form of godliness, but deny the power (2 Timothy 3:5).

A REMARKABLE FEATURE

One remarkable feature in the history of these Philistines was their anxiety to obtain and spoil the most sacred and precious possessions of God's people. I pass over the fact that both Abraham and Isaac were in danger of being robbed of their wives by them (Genesis 20 and 26), for these incidents arose from their own cowardice and want of faith in God; but chapter 21 tells us that they violently took away one of Abraham's wells (21:25), and chapter 26 tells us that they filled up with earth the wells of water that Abraham digged (26:15). They did it because they envied Isaac; it was spiteful and wanton work. Then when Isaac digged other wells they claimed them and strove for them (26:19-21). These wells were essential to the life of the patriarchs and their households, and John chapters 4 and 7 give us the right to interpret them as figuring the Holy Spirit which is given to us, and which is indispensable to the life of God's people now. But what place is there in the carnal religion of our day for the Holy Spirit? Where the superstitions of the ritualists, and the blasphemous criticism and scientific doubt of the modernists prevail, He is a grieved and a quenched Spirit, the wells are filled with earth; nor has the Spirit any place in dead formality, which while boasting in the correctness of its creed has neither faith nor fervour. They seized also the ark of the covenant (1 Samuel 5:2), and were in the land of promise as though it was their own, and Joel 3:5 says of them, *"Ye have taken my silver and gold, and have carried into your temples my goodly and pleasant things."*

The counterpart of this is seen in our day in the fact that men who have not entered the kingdom of God by being born again, but are in it by profession only, are now accepted leaders and teachers in it, and have tacked on to their own philosophical fables the name of Christ, and taken the goodly and pleasant things of our holy faith and attached them to man as he is in his fallen nature, as though there was no necessity for regeneration and redemption, and a new creation in Christ Jesus.

THE FIVE LORDS OF THE PHILISTINES

The Philistines were ruled by five lords (Joshua 13:3; Judges 3:3); and this modern religion is ruled by five lords also, for it is governed by the five senses. Its devotees are controlled by what is natural, and all outside the range of the senses is more or less denied. It is nothing to them that the Scripture saith, *"The natural man receiveth not the things of the Spirit of God: for they are foolishness unto him: neither can he know them, because they are spiritually discerned"* (1 Corinthians 2:14). The natural man is all they are concerned about, for they know no other, and they fulfil this very word by rejecting all that is miraculous in the Word. The incarnation, sacrificial death and resurrection of the Lord Jesus are denied and ridiculed, and His miracles are explained away. Everything that would offend a world that has crucified the Lord of glory, or that the natural man cannot understand or see or feel, is rejected.

It is a remarkable thing that though these people only possessed a very small strip of the land of Canaan, it has taken its name from them, for Palestine means the land of the Philistines, but this name is only given to it in Scripture when the judgment of it is foretold (Exodus 15:14; Isaiah

14:29, 31; Joel 3:4). They came into prominence first in Genesis 21 where they violently robbed Abraham of a well of water, and they were Israel's most persistent foes throughout their history in the land; there is more about them in the Old Testament than any other nation but Israel, and the last mention of them in Scripture is, *"I will cut off the pride of the Philistines"* (Zechariah 9:6). Of the condition of things that is the antitype of them in our day, the Lord has said, *"I will spue thee out of My mouth"* (Revelation 3:16). In the Laodicean Church we see the Philistines in full force.

Rationalism and Ritualism both make their appeal to the natural man who is glad to have his mind inflated and his feelings moved, and they both obscure Christ; indeed He has no place in either. Many a true-hearted disciple entangled in these things and seeing no door of deliverance from them, must be crying out like Mary by the empty sepulchre, *"They have taken away my Lord, and I know not where they have laid Him"* (John 20:13). What can be done?

But is it possible for true Christians to be affected and influenced by that which is so evidently not of God? It is. Christians are often carried away by the plausibility of efforts and teachings which profess to have the uplifting of men in view, when fulcrum and lever of such upliftings are not of God but of men. It is also easy to mistake natural sentiment for true spiritual feeling, and there is the tendency with all to lean on our own understanding instead of the wisdom of God's Spirit. We need to be well grounded in the solemn truth that — "the natural man receiveth not the things of the Spirit of God: for they are foolishness unto him: neither can he know them" (1 Corinthians 2:14). The gospel is not of, nor from men, yet there is nothing else in heaven or earth that can bless them. It is only in the gospel of God's grace that the forgiveness of sins is offered to men. It is divine and from God. It is by the Spirit of God alone that its glories are known, and only those who have received the Spirit can appreciate them.

The Philistines were the most inveterate of all the foes of Israel and held them in bondage during a longer period than any other, and as Israel got weaker in faith their power became greater; nor were they finally overthrown until the supremacy of David — type of Christ in the victory of resurrection — was an established fact in the land.

Israel's Deliverance

In dealing with the deliverance from these people we find at the outset one very remarkable feature. The Israelites in this instance did not raise the cry for deliverance as on former occasions. They seem to have accepted the yoke and become contented with their lot. This became very evident when Samson began to deliver them, for they chided him, saying: "Knowest thou not that the Philistines are rulers over us? what is this that thou hast done unto us?" and they were so completely out of sympathy with all his efforts, that they bound him with cords and brought him to his foes.

Here we have a sad picture of what exists in the present day: the Church has bowed to the domination of these modern Philistines, and, alas! many who are really and truly God's people seem contented to have it so. We may be sure that this state of things does not satisfy those who are truly exercised in heart as to what is for His glory.

It is no small comfort to find, however, that if Israel were indifferent to their own condition the Lord was not, and He set about to deliver them in His own way. The angel of the Lord appeared unto the wife of Manoah, a Danite. She was not the one that men would have chosen. Even her name is not given, and she was a barren woman — a reproach amongst the people of Israel and despised in the eyes of the daughters. But this nameless and despised woman of the meanest of Israel's tribes was the vessel chosen of God, through whom He could work out His own will. Thus we see the great truth emphasized, that His ways are not the ways of men. "I am rich and increased with goods, and have need of nothing", is the vaunting language of secularized Christianity, which walks in the fitful gleam of its own dim light. But "God hath chosen the foolish things of the world ... and things which are despised hath God chosen, yea, and things which are not, to bring to nought things that are: that no flesh should glory in His presence" (1 Corinthians 1:27-29).

"Behold thou art barren and bearest not; but thou shalt conceive and bear a son", was the message from God to the woman, and this message she received in simple and unquestioning faith. Her weakness and reproach are made to stand out boldly, so that it might be manifest that this deliverance was to come from God, and not by the power of man. It was out of weakness, barrenness, and death that God was to bring strength and victory.

But if weakness and reproach marked the woman in the eyes of men, she had perfect and unquestioning faith in God's gracious intentions towards her, and this must have been most precious and acceptable in His sight. Then she was the wife of Manoah, whose name means "rest". Confidence in God and rest of heart are as one; they are securely wedded together, and cannot be divorced.

That confidence in God produces rest of heart was strikingly illustrated in the Apostle Paul. The form of godliness without the power existed in his day, and great havoc was being made by false teachers amongst those for whom he had laboured so zealously. And yet he was not dismayed nor ashamed, for he knew whom he had believed; his trust was in the true David, even Jesus, who had been raised from the dead. So that, while he presents the departure of many from the truth, he is full of rest as to it all.

"Remember", he wrote to his son Timothy, "… Jesus Christ, of the seed of David, … raised from the dead according to my gospel" (2 Timothy 2:8).

If we put side by side his confidence of heart and the things that might have distracted him, as given in the second letter to Timothy, we shall see what resources and strength he had in Jesus Christ.

CHAPTER 1

"This thou knowest, that all they which are in Asia be turned away from me" (verse 15).

"*Nevertheless* I am not ashamed: for I know whom I have believed" (verse 12).

CHAPTER 2

"Their word will eat as doth a canker: … who concerning the truth have erred; … and overthrow the faith of some" (verses 17-18).

"*Nevertheless*, the foundation of God standeth sure, having this seal, The Lord knoweth them that are His" (verse 19).

CHAPTER 3

"Evil men and seducers shall wax worse and worse, deceiving, and being deceived" (verse 13).

"*But* continue thou in the things which thou hast learned … All Scripture is given by inspiration of God, and is profitable for doctrine, for reproof, for correction, for instruction in righteousness" (verses 14, 16).

Chapter 4

"At my first answer no man stood with me, but all men forsook me" (verse 16).

"*Notwithstanding* the Lord stood with me, and strengthened me" (verse 17).

THE GREAT ESSENTIAL

The outstanding feature in the one who was to overthrow the power of the Philistine was Nazariteship. Twice over in the announcement to Manoah's wife the angel of the Lord stated: *the child shall be a Nazarite unto God.* Now a Nazarite had to be separate *from* certain things; but more important than all this was what he was separated *to*. He was to be "unto the Lord", a devoted vessel for the service of God.

He was marked by abstinence from the fruit of the vine, he had to be separate from that which would defile, and his hair had to remain unshorn. These three things we shall also find are made very prominent in Paul's second letter to Timothy.

(1) *The fruit of the vine* is typical, doubtless, of the joys of the natural life, and the Nazarite of today will pay heed to the exhortation: "Thou therefore endure hardness, as a good soldier of Jesus Christ. No man that warreth entangleth himself with the affairs of this life; that he may *please Him* who hath chosen him to be a soldier" (2 Timothy 2:3-4).

(2) *Separation from defilement* is most needful, and the man of God is instructed thereto: "Let every one that nameth the name of Christ depart from iniquity ... If a man therefore purge himself from these, he shall be a vessel unto honour, sanctified, and *meet for the Master's use*, and prepared unto every good work. Flee also youthful lusts" (verses 19-22).

(3) *The unshorn head* was evidently a sign of dependence — of weakness clinging to strength. Long hair is the woman's glory; it is the mark of her dependence as the weaker vessel upon man. This is the place in which God has put her, and true glory is the perfect filling of the place in which one is set. But of the man it is said: "Doth not even nature itself teach you, that, if a man have long hair, it is a shame unto him, forasmuch as he is the image and glory of God" (1 Corinthians 11:7-15). The man's place was to lead; he was made lord of this creation; others were to depend upon him, but he was to rely only upon God. Alas! in the fall he sought to be independent of God; thence all the sorrow and woe and death.

The hair of women is one of the characteristics of those terrible scorpions which will torment men during the period of judgment spoken of in Revelation 9:7-8. They are said to have on their heads crowns like gold, and their faces were as the faces of men, and they had hair as the hair of women. Their first appearance is grand and imposing; they seem to be powerful and independent; but behind all this it is evident that they owe their strength to someone else: they were dependent upon Apollyon the Destroyer (verse 11). The face of the true Nazarite had to be the face of a man: he had to be courageous and unflinching in the presence of the enemy, but he had also to wear the long hair, as the hair of women, for his whole power lay in dependence upon God. This had to be the most prominent of all the features that marked him, even though it became a shame to him in the eyes of others: and if this was lost he became as weak as other men. The Apostle Paul was a true Nazarite when he wrote: "Most gladly therefore will I rather glory in my infirmities, that the power of Christ may rest upon me ... For when I am weak, then am I strong." He had learnt that complete dependence meant true power, for the Lord had said to him: "My grace is sufficient for thee: for My strength is made perfect in weakness" (2 Corinthians 12:9-10). This is surely the *spiritual* teaching for us of the unshorn locks at the Nazarite.

This weakness clinging to the strength of the Lord is clearly seen in 2 Timothy: "Thou therefore, my son, be strong in the grace that is in Christ Jesus" (2:1). "Out of them all the Lord delivered me" (3:11). "The Lord stood with me" (4:17).

THE LORD JESUS OUR PERFECT EXAMPLE

The Lord Jesus was the true Nazarite, wholly devoted to God. He was never hindered in His willing service by the comforts and joys which belong to this life. He had no shelter but a shed and no cradle but a manger when He came into the world. The foxes had their holes and the birds of the air their nests, but He had neither home nor resting place on earth. He always refused to be influenced by those who would have chosen for Him an easier, and in their eyes more natural path.

He walked spotless and undefiled through the world: sore temptations constantly beset Him, but He was never ensnared; the sinful things that attracted other men had no charm for Him. He was ever and wholly separate from sinners, and wholly consecrated to the will of God.

Then, lastly, He was ever the absolutely dependent One. His language was: "He wakeneth morning by morning:

He wakeneth My ear to hear as the learner" (Isaiah 50:4). In all He did and said He was instructed by His Father, whose will He came to do day by day. This will was accomplished; no more, no less. His meat was to do His Father's will. He had no motive for living except His Father's glory, and all through His earthly life He was completely and altogether dependent upon God, so that He could say: "I was cast upon Thee from the womb" (Psalm 22:10). There is in Him sufficient grace to enable us to walk in His steps, and as we do so the victorious life of Nazariteship will be ours.

NAZARITESHIP WAS SAMSON'S STRENGTH

As long as he maintained this inviolate he was a suited vessel for the power of God, and in the first freshness and strength of this he is a faint foreshadowing of Christ and His work.

Bear in mind that Samson came into the world for the express purpose of overthrowing the Philistines and thus setting God's people free; and, seeing that this was his mission, it is not surprising that a young lion — typical of Satan's power — roared against him.

But Samson was more than a match for the lion, and rent it as one would rend a kid. In like manner all the powers of darkness gathered against the Lord Jesus Christ, for He came to expose all that was false and to establish all that was true. But, in death He gained the victory; by dying he overthrew the foe; and, just as the carcass of Samson's lion yielded meat and sweetness, so the death of Jesus yields life and nourishment for the soul, and true joy for the heart. We see the reality and faithfulness of divine love displayed in that great conflict and victory, and we owe our every blessing to it.

The honey was in his hand (Judges 14:9)

The hand that smote the lion held the honey, and Samson shared it, the remarkable fruit of his victory, with his parents, as they walked in company with him.

The great antitype of this should yield abundant joy to us. *All blessing is held in the mighty hand that smote the power of death*, and it is the delight of our Lord Jesus Christ to dispense to us of that which He holds so securely.

Some in the vanity of their imaginations would have us believe that salvation, and indeed every blessing, has been deposited in the Church for us, and that we can neither know nor realize these things apart from it. Alas, for us, if this were so; for the Church as a responsible vessel of testimony here has utterly failed, for it has joined hands with the world that refused the Lord. But Christ can never fail: He has risen up victoriously above all the ruin and wreck which sin and death have made, and all the promises of God are "yea and amen" in Him, and as we cleave to Him we shall have our hearts nourished and made glad by the sweet fruits of His death.

The Philistines who came to the wedding feast (chapter 14:10-19), and were only nominally attached to Samson, did not taste the honey from the lion's carcass, and the whole matter was nothing more than a riddle to them. These Philistines represent those to whom reference has already been made, who are professors without possession, who have accepted the form of Christianity without the power. To all such the truth of God is but so many doctrines to be discussed and riddles to be solved: for "the natural man receiveth not the things of the Spirit of God: for they are foolishness unto him: neither can he know them, because they are spiritually discerned" (1 Corinthians 2:14). There is nothing in the death of

Christ that appeals to such; they cannot understand blessing coming out of death; they cannot see how meat can come forth from the eater, or sweetness from the strong one. "Christ crucified, [is] unto the Jews a stumbling block, and unto the Greeks foolishness" (1 Corinthians 1:23).

But that which is a perfect enigma to unrenewed men, be they religious or wise, is to us who are saved the power and the wisdom of God. The mighty eater — death — has been made to yield us meat, and out of the strong one has come forth sweetness; for the full glory of God's all-conquering and unchanging love has shone forth in the death of Jesus. God's wisdom and power were there seen in all their greatness, and the souls of those who see these things are saved and satisfied. Too much emphasis cannot be laid upon this, for it is only as we are living in the reality of these things that we shall overcome the Philistines; there is always the danger, even with those who are truly converted, of occupation with doctrine only. We must have correct doctrine and hold fast the form of sound words, but we must know what is at the back of the words and what the realities are which the doctrines express. Many are wasting time in seeking to elucidate knotty questions and discussing dogmas, and all the while losing the sweet honey that may be enjoyed in company with the Lord. This riddle-solving is dry and unprofitable work; that we may feast upon the honey is the Lord's desire for us.

THE PHILISTINES' INTENTION

The next important event in Samson's history was the attempt of the Philistines to make him a prisoner. They found that he would make no compromise with them. He was an open and determined foe, so they "went up, and pitched in Judah, and spread themselves in Lehi. And the men of Judah said, Why are ye come up against us? And they answered, To bind Samson are we come up" (chapter 15:9-10). *To bind the Nazarite* and thus render him helpless was their object. Satan works today upon similar lines; and the existing lifeless counterfeit of true Christianity shows only too plainly how successful he has been.

It is distressing to see that the men of Judah put themselves in league with the Philistines in this purpose: they had no desire to be free from their yoke: they looked upon Samson as a disturber of their peace and chided him, saying: "Knowest thou not that the Philistines are rulers over us. What is this that thou hast done to us?" But is not this also the tendency of the day? If any man raises a voice of warning against the evil doctrines or worldly practices that abound, he is looked upon as a disturber, his mouth must be closed, he must be bound and curbed. He will be told that it is wrong to go to extremes; that moderation is the great desideratum. But, judged by that standard, a lukewarm temperature is justified, and fire stands condemned, for it is extremely hot. But what saith the Lord? "I know thy works, that thou art neither cold nor hot. ... So then because thou art lukewarm, and neither cold nor hot, I will spue thee out of my mouth" (Revelation 3:15-16).

Christians, we need to awake to righteousness. We need to be stirred up and filled with a fervour of devotion to Christ, that will consume every new cord with which an indifferent profession would bind us, so that unfettered we may earnestly contend for the faith once delivered to the saints, and so remain true to our Lord.

THE PLACE OF POWER

But Samson dwelt in the top of the rock Etam. It is true that he allowed his brethren to bind him for a time, but when the Spirit of the Lord came upon him, their fetters perished as flax in the fire, and with the jawbone of an ass he slew a thousand men. The top of the rock is evidently the place from whence to get the victory. It stands for stability and strength; that which is immovable, and upon which the storms must beat in vain. Our Lord has become a rock to us. He has laid a foundation broad and deep, and no assault or storm can shake that foundation. He who builds thereon is safe for ever. The rock is Himself. All the thoughts and intentions of God are secured in Him, as the One raised up from the dead — "who hath abolished death, and brought life and incorruptibility to light through the gospel" (2 Timothy 1:10).

If we would be victorious we must cleave closely to Him in this blessed character: and so shall we be preserved from depression and defeat. Moreover, it is only as we prove the reality of His power and grace that we are kept free of that which is but an empty counterfeit: and knowing whom we have believed are confident that the foundation of God standeth sure in spite of all attempts to overthrow it (2 Timothy 1:12; 2:19). Then shall we be able in meekness to instruct those who have fallen into this snare of the devil — religion without reality — and the result may be that they will acknowledge the truth (2 Timothy 2:25-26).

It has often been remarked that the moment of victory is the moment of greatest weakness, and Samson felt this. He was sore athirst, and called on the LORD, and said: "Thou hast given this great deliverance into the hand of Thy servant: and now shall I die for thirst, and fall into the hand of the uncircumcised?" (Judges 15:18). This was his fear: to fall into the hands of the uncircumcised, to be in their power. Now the Philistines are constantly spoken of in this way. Circumcision, which speaks of the cutting off and setting aside of the flesh, had no place with them; and, this being the case, it was right that the Nazarite should fear coming under their power. Would that there were more of this fear today; it would make us more like Samson in his dependence upon God.

How the Victorious Life is Maintained

But God had a provision for His fainting but dependent servant: it was the well of water.

"But God clave an hollow place that was in the jaw [in Lehi], and there came water thereout; and when he had drunk, his spirit came again, and he revived: wherefore he called the name thereof En-hakkore" (chapter 15:19), which means "the well of him that cried". This is not the first time in Scripture that the water and the rock are found together. Both are necessary for us, for it is by the water, which sets forth for us life in the power of the Spirit, that the life of the Nazarite is maintained in freshness and vigour.

"In the last day, that great day of the feast, Jesus stood and cried, saying, If any man thirst, let him come unto Me, and drink. He that believeth on Me, as the Scripture hath said, out of his belly shall flow rivers of living water. But this spake He of the Spirit, which they that believe on Him should receive: for the Holy Ghost was not yet given; because that Jesus was not yet glorified" (John 7:37-39).

Here is the provision for maintenance of the life of the Nazarite; for it is by the Spirit of God that the soul is kept in touch with the things of Christ, the new life is maintained in its freshness and vigour, and the Nazarite is renewed day by day. Then by the same Spirit is given power to help others.

Samson judged Israel for twenty years. Though the Philistines were there, he maintained what was for God throughout that period.

Do we desire to contend boldly for the truth, to stand for Christ, keeping His Word and not denying His Name? Then three things are absolutely needful:—

(1)   Nazariteship — Devotion to the Lord.

(2)   The Rock — The knowledge of perfect stability of all God's purposes in Christ risen from the dead.

(3)   The well of water — Dependence on the Spirit of God for refreshment of soul and power for service.

THE LOSS OF NAZARITESHIP

Now we turn from Samson's victories to his terrible defeat. The sad and shameful story is not hidden from us, for God would teach us not only how to tread the path of victory, but also make plain for our warning the terrible results of departure from Him, so that we may not trust in ourselves.

"Then went Samson to Gaza" (Judges 16:1).

Here is the commencement of that downward course. It is true that he survived at Gaza, though the Gazites were determined to slay him. He had not then surrendered his Nazariteship and he still proved stronger than the Philistines' strength, which is the meaning of Gaza. He took the gate and pillars, with the bar, and bore them away to the top of the hill that is before Hebron.

But self-confidence seemed to mark him, and he must have forgotten that his strength was in dependence upon God. He heeded not the warning that his escape from Gaza ought to have been to him, for it came to pass afterwards that he loved a woman in the valley — or by the brook [AV margin] — of Sorek, whose name was Delilah (verse 4).

Sorek means "the vine", and it is most pitiful to see the victorious Nazarite, who had dwelt upon the rock and drank of the well there, now going down to drink of the brook which flowed through the valley of the vines. As the Nazarite he had refused the fruit of the vine, and at the commencement of his career he had slain a lion in the vineyards. There he overcame the strong one. Now in the valley of the vines he falls a victim to Delilah, whose name means weakness.

Here are the downward steps:—

> He loved a woman in the valley of Sorek (verse 4).
>
> He told her all his heart (verse 17).
>
> She made him sleep upon her knees (verse 19).
>
> The seven locks of his head were shorn (verse 19).
>
> The Lord departed from him (verse 20).
>
> The Philistines took him (verse 21).
>
> They put out his eyes, bound him with fetters of brass, and he did grind in the prison house (verse 21).

This was the depth of degradation to which his departure from God brought him. The one whose name means "As the sun" is seen grinding for the enemies of the Lord in the blindness and darkness of his lost Nazariteship.

There is one mention of a prison in Scripture before this. Joseph was cast into it because he stood firm in his devotion to God and his determination not to sin against Him. That devotion meant much suffering, but it was the path of victory. Here is a woeful contrast. Joseph's prison meant victory; Samson's prison spelt utter defeat. What a host of Philistines and all their strength had failed to accomplish, his own unbridled desire had brought about. The one who had delivered his brethren from the Philistines was bound by them. God's Nazarite became the devil's slave. He who carried away the gates of Gaza is led back through those gates as a prisoner, and the one who had made his foes to quake and flee now makes laughter for them at the festival of their god. If we found encouragement in Samson's exploits, learning from them what an individual, when in dependence upon God, can accomplish, we are now warned against self-confidence by seeing how low the strong man may fall.

If we would escape such defeat we must know wherein our strength lies; we must know the secret of En-hakkore — "the well of him that called" — which secret is dependence upon God and the judgment of self.

Remember, it was not the strength of the Philistines which overcame Samson. He was drawn away from the path of devotion to God by their seductions. It was not fear of their anger that vanquished him. He was beguiled and ensnared by the smiles of Delilah; he was betrayed by their apparent friendship. The devil's desire is to beguile all who are true to the Lord, to ensnare them by that which is not of God. This is what Paul feared for God's people when he wrote: "I am jealous over you with godly jealousy: for I have espoused you to one husband, that I may present you as a chaste virgin to Christ. But I fear, lest by any means, as the serpent beguiled Eve through his subtilty, so your minds should be corrupted from the simplicity that is in Christ" (2 Corinthians 11:2-3). And this danger is greater than ever in these last days.

Yes, it is possible for the Nazarite to fall; it is possible for those who have lived the unfettered life of devotion to the Lord to become bound by the brazen chains of a lifeless and formal religion; it is even possible to find such grinding at the mills of a scornful and God-rejecting world. There are those who were once eminent for their true heart-separation from the friendship of the world who are now found associated with it — linked up with those who despise the Cross of Christ and deny its virtue — in the furtherance of schemes and policies in which God has no part. They build again that which they destroyed, and serve that against which they contended, and without question they make sport for that which they serve. "Ye adulterers and adulteresses, know ye not that the friendship of the world is enmity with God? whosoever therefore will be a friend of the world is the enemy of God" (James 4:4). These are scathing words for such, nor dare we tone them down. There they stand in all their trenchant power: our business is to pay heed to them.

The consequence of this spiritual adultery, this going down to compromise with the world, is loss of spiritual sight and power.

"Her Nazarites were purer than snow, they were whiter than milk, they were more ruddy in body than rubies, their polishing was of sapphire." But their purity is gone; they are defiled and polluted. "Their visage is blacker than a coal; they are not known in the streets: their skin cleaveth to their bones; it is withered, it is become like a stick" (Lamentations 4:7-8).

A GREAT RECOVERY

But just as the child learns the character of fire by being burnt, and refuses to touch it henceforward, so the people of God often learn lessons of great value through their failure; and thus God triumphs and good comes out of evil.

It was so in Samson's case. In his captivity he felt the treachery of Delilah's friendship, and turned to the Lord. "His hair began to grow" (Judges 16:22). He judged that which had blinded and enfeebled him, and took up a most uncompromising attitude towards it, with the result that he gained a greater victory than had been possible at any time during his brightest days. It meant death to himself; nevertheless the victory was great and real.

It is a great comfort to remember that the Lord changes not, and that He is ever ready to forgive and restore.

> *"Still sweet 'tis to discover,*
> *If clouds have dimmed my sight,*
> *When passed, Eternal Lover,*
> *Towards me, as e'er, Thou'rt bright."*

The grace of the Lord is greater than all the sin of His people. His quenchless love burns towards them in all its brightness, and cannot grow dim. He is the same yesterday, today, and for ever.

If we have been ensnared by the world into conformity with it — if we have been induced to step down from the highway of single-eyed devotion to the Lord and undivided dependence upon Him, to toy with the world, and have felt the bitterness of so doing, here is encouragement for us. He who was not deaf to the prayer of Samson will listen to our cry, and He will give deliverance and victory.

But the *self* within us that was ensnared by the world must be judged by us as well as the world that ensnared us. This surely is the lesson that the death of Samson would teach us.

To judge the world and self means to turn away from both completely to the Lord alone. This was the path that Paul trod. He had to withstand Peter, who left the place of the Nazarite to grind at the mill of a legal and fleshly religion

(Galatians 2:11-14). But for himself he says: "God forbid that I should glory, save in the cross of our Lord Jesus Christ, by whom the world is crucified unto me, and I unto the world" (Galatians 6:14).

There was the end of the religious world and the Paul who might be ensnared by it. The Cross of Christ had disclosed the true character of both, while the greatness of the love that the Cross revealed had made Paul a Nazarite for ever; and, if a Nazarite, a triumphant and joyous man; for the Nazarite is invincible as long as he maintains his Nazariteship. That path is open to all. It may mean persecution and rejection by the world; for those who take this path will surely be scoffed at as being bigoted and narrow, and they may even have to bear the marks of the Lord Jesus in their body (Galatians 6:17); but the final triumph, the crown of righteousness, and the smile of the Lord are at the end of the conflict. He hath said, "To him that overcometh will I grant to sit with Me in My throne, even as I also overcame, and am set down with My Father in His throne. He that hath an ear, let him hear what the Spirit saith unto the churches" (Revelation 3:21-22).

Delivered and Devoted

"And Ruth said, Intreat me not to leave thee, or to return from following after thee: for whither thou goest, I will go; and where thou lodgest, I will lodge: thy people shall be my people, and thy God my God: Where thou diest, will I die, and there will I be buried: the LORD do so to me, and more also, if ought but death part thee and me. When she saw that she was stedfastly minded to go with her, then she left speaking unto her. So they two went until they came to Bethlehem. And it came to pass, when they were come to Bethlehem, that all the city was moved about them, and they said, Is this Naomi? And she said unto them, Call me not Naomi, call me Mara: for the Almighty hath dealt very bitterly with me."

RUTH 1:16-20

"And the women said unto Naomi, Blessed be the LORD, which hath not left thee this day without a kinsman, that his name may be famous in Israel. And he shall be unto thee a restorer of thy life, and a nourisher of thine old age: for thy daughter in law, which loveth thee, which is better to thee than seven sons, hath born him. And Naomi took the child, and laid it in her bosom, and became nurse unto it. And the women her neighbours gave it a name, saying, There is a son born to Naomi; and they called his name Obed: he is the father of Jesse, the father of David."

RUTH 4:14-17

Chapter 7
Delivered and Devoted

NO KING IN ISRAEL

The closing chapters of Judges bring out in startling fashion the quick descent of Israel from their faithfulness to God. When once upon the down grade their progress was rapid, and the terrible terminus was marked by covetousness, apostasy, corruption, and mutual destruction. It is stated in connection with each of these things that "there was no king in Israel", and "every man did that which was right in his own eyes" (Judges 21:25). The sad results depicted were the only possible outcome of the lawlessness and self-pleasing which characterized the people at that time.

God has ordained kings and governors for the good of men, because it is necessary that they should be ruled and controlled, and those who would live lives of peace and tranquility in this world must be subject to the powers that be. But these rulers are representative of that which is higher and greater, even of God Himself. He is the great Ruler — the King Immortal; and subjection to Him means peace and blessing for men. His yoke has been cast off, alas, for sin is rebellion against God, and lawlessness has taken the place of His just rule in the lives of men. This is true of all naturally, for the Scripture saith: "All we like sheep have gone astray; we have turned every one to his own way" (Isaiah 53:6). And again: "All have sinned, and come short of the glory of God" (Romans 3:23).

In the face of these facts how glorious is the news that God has found a righteous way of blessing sinners — that He is graciously calling men back to Himself — and that all who obey His call are pardoned and saved; and, instead of walking in the paths of destruction and death, are led by Him in the paths of righteousness and life.

They "sought an inheritance to dwell in" (Judges 18)

Covetousness and discontent, as well as lawlessness, flourished in the midst of Israel; for we find a Levite who was prepared to sell his God and his people for silver; and a tribe which, not content with the inheritance of the Lord, sought out a place for themselves. In both instances apostasy from God was the consequence. It was His intention to be King in Israel: His rule would have been most beneficent, and every man in the land would have been satisfied with the fatness thereof. But the children of Jacob loved their own way instead of His, and these Danites thought they could seek out for themselves that which would be better than what God had for them. It is a remarkable fact that no mention is made of them amongst the 144,000 of Israel who will yet stand before God to sing of His salvation (Revelation 7).

It is sad enough to see these things in men who do not know God: it is doubly sad to see them in those who have professed to belong to Him; but history repeats itself, and that which was true of Israel of old is, alas, only too true of many who have professed to know God today; and it is most certain that nothing can keep men from being carried with the down-grade stream of independence and self-pleasing, and of apostasy from the truth of God's gospel which is running so strongly today, but the vital knowledge of Christ as Saviour and Lord.

There are those who boast of a godly ancestry; or association with religious bodies of repute and antiquity; or with Christians whose doctrines are Scriptural; but none of these things will put or keep us right; there must be living, saving faith in our Lord Jesus Christ, and constant and personal devotion to Him. It is very significant that the apostate Danites came out of the city of Samson. They knew and had seen his mighty exploits as God's devoted Nazarite, but this did not keep them from wholesale departure from God; and the leader of the apostasy was none other than the grandson of Moses. *

A Great Contrast

In the ancient Jewish Scriptures the Book of Ruth formed part of the Book of Judges. The events therein recorded took place during the period in which the Judges lived, and Ruth's life and devotion form a pleasing contrast to the sad apostasy that marked the end of those times.

She is a true type of undivided devotion to one well-beloved object; for, delivered from every entanglement in the land of Moab by the love of Naomi, she was altogether controlled by that love which had set her free. Now the result of deliverance is devotion to the Deliverer, and the Lord desires to set us free from the world, the flesh, and the devil, and everything that binds us, so that we may follow Him alone. He would bind us to Himself by the strong fetters of love, and reign supreme in our affections, as Naomi did in the heart of Ruth. This is the end of all

---

* It is generally admitted that Judges 18:30 should read: "Jonathan, the son of Gershom, the son of Moses."

overcoming; to this our talks should lead; and this will be of greater value in His sight than mighty exploits, and a greater victory over Satan than any work could be.

NAOMI AND MARA

Naomi exhibited certain traits which have come out in all their perfection in Jesus, and the path which she trod is in certain respects illustrative of His sorrow and travail and its resultant joy.

She went into a far away land and there tasted the bitterness of death, insomuch that she had to cry: "Call me not Naomi [which means 'pleasant'] but Mara [which means 'bitterness.']." But, in the midst of the sorrow through which she passed, she must have displayed something of the sweetness of which her name spoke, for only in this way can we account for Ruth's devotion to her.

Sweetness and bitterness met in Naomi, but if we could see these things in all their perfection and intensity we must turn to Jesus. His name is sweet, the sweetest our ears have ever heard, and He is altogether pleasant to those whose eyes have been opened by the grace of God. He was so when here on earth; He is just the same upon the throne today; but we could never have known the sweetness that abides in Him if He had not trodden the path of bitterness and sorrow. He was the Man of tears, the Man of the broken heart (Psalm 69); but the grief of that wonderful life of sweetest devotion to God, and love to men, was but the preliminary to the awful sorrow that He endured on the cross, when He took the bitter cup of sin's judgment from the hand of God. It was then that the waterfloods rolled over Him, and every sorrow found its centre in His blessed heart. Calvary spelt "Mara" for Jesus; but the intensity of that bitterness only disclosed the sweetness of that marvellous love which no power could check nor sorrow overwhelm. Yes, His is an unmeasured love; stronger than death, more lasting than the ages, unutterably sweet.

It was to Naomi in her sorrow that Ruth clung, and for the love of her who had passed through "Mara" she said: "Intreat me not to leave thee, or to return from following after thee: for whither thou goest, I will go; and where thou lodgest, I will lodge: thy people shall be my people, and thy God my God: where thou diest, will I die, and there will I be buried: the LORD do so to me, and more also, if ought but death part thee and me" (Ruth 1:16-17).

When she made this memorable decision she knew nothing of Boaz, type of Christ in His present position of power, nor of the place of favour and exaltation that awaited her. The love of Naomi controlled her and she was satisfied, be it noted, not to dwell and to live, but to "lodge" and to "die" with Naomi. She embraced the path of strangership for the compensation that she found in the pleasantness of Naomi's company.

How true are the words —

> *"'Tis the treasure we've found in His love*
> *Which has made us now pilgrims below."*

Nothing else will: the thought of coming glories will not, in itself, separate us from the world. The attractions of the "world to come", and its attractions are indeed great, will not of themselves draw our hearts out of "this present evil world". His love alone — the love displayed at Calvary — can do this: and so the path of discipleship is invariably connected with the cross. It was this that controlled the apostle, for he said: "The life which I now live in the flesh I live by the faith of the Son of God, *who loved me and gave Himself for me*" (Galatians 2:20).

God grant that just as the portion that Ruth found in Naomi delivered her from Moab for ever, and bound her up with the interests of the one whose love controlled her, so may the preciousness of Jesus, who endured the cross and despised the shame, constrain us to wholehearted devotion to Himself.

THE RESULT OF FOLLOWING THE LORD

Ruth lost nothing by cleaving to Naomi, for, as a result of it, "Her hap was to light on a part of the field belonging unto Boaz" (Ruth 2:3); and he was a man of tender heart, for he spake kindly to Ruth and comforted her (verse 13). But not only so: he was a mighty man of wealth, and the field over which he had power was altogether sufficient to satisfy her need.

If we consider Naomi's sorrow as illustrating the deep and sore travail through which the Lord Himself passed, the wealth of Boaz will speak to us of His present greatness and power. He has been highly exalted; all things have been put into His hand; and now He finds great delight in dispensing the blessings of God to those who are poor and needy.

Boaz would not have said, "Go not to glean in another field", unless he had known that his field was sufficient for Ruth; nor would the Lord have said, "My grace is sufficient for thee", if its fulness could not meet our every need.

Are there steep places in the path of discipleship, and do trials beset the feet of the pilgrim? The grace of the Lord is greater than all, and those who tread the path prove the blessedness of it, for He has said that they "shall ... *receive manifold more in this present time*, and in the world to come life everlasting" (Luke 18:30).

So Ruth gleaned in the fields of Boaz as long as gleaning was needful, and she found that he cared for her in every way, so that she was not only satisfied herself but had also something to spare.

The whole story is of deepest interest and full of instruction; but we must now pass on to the end of the book.

The results of Naomi's sorrow

It is remarkable that at the end of the story Naomi is again the prominent person; not now in bitterness and sorrow, but reaping the pleasant fruits of her travail.

(1) The Church

She had lost Elimelech and her sons in the land of Moab, but she had gained Ruth, who was better to her than seven sons (chapter 4:15), and in this we have a figure of what the Lord has lost and gained by His death. He came to His own people Israel, but they rejected Him, and for the time being He lost the kingdom and the nation; He was cut off out of the land of the living. But if He lost Israel for a while, He gained the Church; and no tongue can tell how precious the Church is to Him. It is the "pearl of great price" for which He sold all that He had, and for which He went down into the deep sea of death, when the midnight darkness of God's judgment rested upon the face of it.

> *"Down beneath those sunless waters*
>   *He from heaven has passed;*
> *There He found His heart's desire,*
>   *Found His pearl at last.*
> *All He had His heart has given*
>   *For this gem unpriced —*
> *This the tale of love unfathomed,*
>   *This the love of Christ."*

I do not here speak of the outward profession of the Name of Christ, which has become so corrupted, but of what is real in it, that which He calls "My Church".

The Church as the Lamb's wife will be His eternal companion, for the time is not far distant when there shall sound "as it were the voice of a great multitude, and as the voice of many waters, and as the voice of many thunderings, saying, Alleluia: for the Lord God omnipotent reigneth. Let us be glad and rejoice, and give honour to Him: for the marriage of the Lamb is come, and His wife hath made herself ready" (Revelation 19:6-7). Then in that glorious consummation the Lord shall see of His soul's deep travail and be satisfied; but even now, whilst He is rejected from the earth, the Church is His consolation and joy.

Is it not strange that some who belong to His Church — every blood-bought believer is a member of it — should seek the smiles of the world that rejected Him, instead of seeking only to fill the high privilege of giving joy to His heart? No higher privilege will be ours for ever; no greater loss could befall us, as Christians, than the loss of it. It is this which the devil seeks to mar and spoil, and for this he plies his wiles and spreads his snares, and the true overcomer is the one who, cleaving to the Lord alone, is glad to lose all for Himself.

(2) Worship for the Father

The women of Bethlehem gathered round Naomi to felicitate her upon the joy that was hers, and they say: "There is a son born to Naomi" (chapter 4:17). They do not say born unto Boaz or to Ruth; but to Naomi, for the child would never have been but for that sore "Mara" in the distant land.

And the women gave this child, which they counted as Naomi's son, a name, and "they called his name Obed", the meaning of which is "worshipping God". "And Naomi took the child, and laid it in her bosom, and became nurse unto it" (4:16). The child was greatly beloved by her, for it was the fruit of Ruth, who loved her (4:15).

Here is set forth another result of the death of the Lord Jesus. He came forth from the Father because the Father sought worshippers (John 4:23). And for this He suffered and died: and in this respect His death has not been in vain, for by that death He has brought a countless host to God, all ransomed by His precious blood. These can worship God in spirit and in truth, for they know His love as it has been declared in the death of Christ.

Who can tell the joy that fills the heart of the Lord as He presents the worship of those who love Him to God the Father? Such worship, rendered from hearts filled by the love of God, is very precious to Jesus, for it is the fruit of the hearts and lips of those who love Him and whom He loves.

(3) Kingly glory for Christ

Ruth and Obed were followed by Jesse and David; and David as the king typified the coming glory of Christ.

The Lord is still rejected by this world, but the time of His return is at hand; the crown of universal dominion shall encircle His once thorn-pierced brow, and as great David's greater Son He shall sway the sceptre from the river unto the ends of the earth. Then shall Israel own Him as the Son of God and their King, and the groanings of a sin-blighted earth shall be hushed, and everything that hath breath will break forth into singing, and every note of every song shall be in praise of the King.

How deep will be the joy of His heart when He looks abroad upon a creation which has been made to smile by the light of His countenance, and when men, delivered from the thraldom of Satan's power, shall rejoice in the knowledge of God! But the foundation of all the gladness which will mantle the earth in the day of His kingly glory is His sorrow and death.

All who love Him earnestly desire this day of glory, and rejoice in the blessed fact that He shall be exalted and adored in the very world in which He was despised and put to shame. But not because of the crowns of an endless glory that shall shine upon His sacred brow do we love and follow Him, but because of His love, love that disclosed its sweetness amid the shame and grief of Calvary's "Mara". It is this love, and this alone, that constrains us to serve Him untiringly, follow Him devotedly, and love Him now with fervent and undivided heart. This is the pathway of the overcomer.

Is it our desire to tread this path? Then let us hold it fast, for He hath said: "Behold, I come quickly: hold that fast which thou hast, that no man take thy crown. *Him that overcometh* will I make a pillar in the temple of My God, and he shall go no more out: and I will write upon him the name of My God, and the name of the city of My God, which is new Jerusalem, which cometh down out of heaven from My God: and I will write upon him My new name. He that hath an ear, let him hear what the Spirit saith unto the churches" (Revelation 3:11-13).

HOW TO OVERCOME

OTHER BOOKS FROM SCRIPTURE TRUTH PUBLICATIONS

NEW TESTAMENT COMMENTARY SERIES BY F. B. HOLE:

THE GOSPELS AND ACTS
ISBN 978-0-901860-42-2 (paperback)
ISBN 978-0-901860-46-0 (hardback)
392 pages; February 2007

ROMANS AND CORINTHIANS
ISBN 978-0-901860-43-9 (paperback)
ISBN 978-0-901860-47-7 (hardback)
176 pages; February 2007

GALATIANS TO PHILEMON
ISBN 978-0-901860-44-6 (paperback)
ISBN 978-0-901860-48-4 (hardback)
204 pages; February 2007

HEBREWS TO REVELATION
ISBN 978-0-901860-45-3 (paperback)
ISBN 978-0-901860-49-1 (hardback)
304 pages; February 2007

UNDERSTANDING CHRISTIANITY SERIES:

SEEK YE FIRST BY JOHN S BLACKBURN
ISBN 978-0-901860-61-3 (paperback)
ISBN 978-0-901860-02-6 (hardback)
136 pages; February 2007

GOD'S INSPIRATION OF THE SCRIPTURES BY WILLIAM KELLY
ISBN 978-0-901860-51-4 (paperback)
ISBN 978-0-901860-56-9 (hardback)
484 pages; March 2007

LECTURES ON THE CHURCH OF GOD BY WILLIAM KELLY
ISBN 978-0-901860-50-7 (paperback)
244 pages; February 2007
ISBN 978-0-901860-55-2 (hardback)
244 pages; March 2007

UNDERSTANDING THE OLD TESTAMENT SERIES:
DELIVERING GRACE BY JOHN T MAWSON
ISBN 978-0-901860-64-4 (paperback)
ISBN 978-0-901860-78-1 (hardback)
192 pages; March 2007

ELIJAH: A PROPHET OF THE LORD BY HAMILTON SMITH
ISBN 978-0-901860-68-2 (paperback)
80 pages; March 2007

ELISHA: THE MAN OF GOD BY HAMILTON SMITH
ISBN 978-0-901860-79-8 (paperback)
92 pages; March 2007

THE GOSPEL IN JOB BY YANNICK FORD
ISBN 978-0-901860-76-7 (paperback)
ISBN 978-0-901860-77-4 (hardback)
112 pages; March 2007

LESSONS FROM EZRA BY TED MURRAY
ISBN 978-0-901860-75-0 (paperback)
84 pages; March 2007

LESSONS FROM NEHEMIAH BY TED MURRAY
ISBN 978-0-901860-86-6 (paperback)
124 pages; August 2008

Printed in the United States
141871LV00001B/18/P